Copyright © 2008 by Bramcost Publications
All rights reserved
Published in the United States of America

This Bramcost Publications edition is an unabridged republication
of the rare original work first published in 1925.

www.BramcostPublications.com

ISBN 10: 1-934268-88-7
ISBN 13: 978-1-934268-88-9

Library of Congress Control Number: 2009920384

From painting by Winterhalter

Empress Eugenie

HATS
AND HOW TO MAKE THEM

By
VIRGINIA C. PATTY
*Assistant Professor in Home Economics, University of Washington,
Seattle, Washington*

THE CONTENTS

	PAGE
The Preface	xi

PART I. CHARACTER IN A HAT

CHAPTER
- I. THE CHOICE OF A HAT 1
    Selection Often Difficult—Test of a Becoming Hat—Color and Texture

PART II. PAPER PATTERNS

- II. HOW TO MAKE PAPER PATTERNS 10
    Brim Copying—Brim Designing—Paper Brim Construction—Crown Designing—Paper Crown Construction

PART III. EQUIPMENT AND MATERIALS

- III. EQUIPMENT 26
- IV. MATERIALS FOR CONSTRUCTION 32
    Braids—Fabrics—Furs

PART IV. MAKING THE HAT

- V. MOLDED FRAMES 42
    Materials—Placing Pattern on Willow—Headsize—Shaping Brim—Molding Brims without Patterns—Crowns
- VI. WIRE FRAMES 53
    Materials — Measurements — Construction — Headsize Wire — Support or Spoke Wires—Sailor Frame—Mushroom or Drooping Brim—Upturning or Rolling Brim—Upturning Brim with Slash on Side—Mold for Irregular Shape—Covering Frame—Molding Willow over Wire—Molding over Paper—Wire Crown Molds and Frames
- VII. ESTIMATING MATERIALS FOR HAT COVERINGS 70
    Measuring for Brims—Measuring for Crowns—Covering Frame—Covering Irregular Shapes

THE CONTENTS

VIII. COVERING CROWNS 78
    Crown Drawn Tightly over Foundation—Plain Crown in Two Pieces—Soft Crowns, Two—Sectional Crown—Attaching Brim to Crown—Finishing at Base with Cord

IX. COVERING HAT WITH BRAIDS 83
    Sewing Braids—Preparation of Braids—Frames for Braids—Covering Brim—Making Crowns—Sewing Braids over Wire Mold—Removing Brim from Mold

X. STITCHES AND PROCESSES USED IN CONSTRUCTION OF HATS . . 91

XI. EDGE FINISHES AND BINDINGS 95
    Bias Folds—Flat Folds—French or Milliner's Fold—Bias Fold on Edge of Brim—Fold on Edge of Brim without a Wire—Fold Made before Attaching—Narrow Ribbon or Braid Binding on Edge—Narrow Bindings of Silk or Organdy—Combination of Brim Covering and Binding—Plain Bias Fold Extending beyond Edge of Brim—Plain Edge—Shirred Edges, Three—Sectional Facings—Cord Finishing

XII. TYPES OF HATS AND THEIR CONSTRUCTION 106
    Making the Sports Hat—Soft Hat of Bias Folds—Bias Folds with Running Stitch for Decorating—Bias Folds Decorated with Narrow Hemp Braid and Running Stitches—Crown of Bias Folds—Hats Made from Strips of Silk or Ribbon with Cord Edge—Crown with a Wire Cord—Underfacing of Radiating Strips with a Cord Edge—Ribbon Hats, Three—Making Brim with Cords—Shirred Hat of Silk—Silk Hat Stitched or Hemstitched—Tucked Brim—Halo Brims, Two—Child's Stitched Hat—Tam-o'-Shanters, Eight

PART V. TRIMMING THE HAT

XIII. HANDMADE TRIMMINGS 123
    Bows—Rosette—Ribbon Cockade with Variations—Cord Trimmings—Novelty Trimmings—Flowers and Fruit

XIV. DECORATIVE STITCHES AND PROCESSES 156

XV. FEATHERS 160
    Laws Governing Use of Feathers—Kinds

XVI. HAT LININGS 164
    Directions for Making

THE CONTENTS

PART VI. RENOVATION AND CARE OF HAT

XVII. RENOVATION AND CARE 166

    Handling the Hat—General Upkeep or Care—Freshening Straw Hats—Reshaping Frames—Varying the Style of Crown—Renovating Materials

PART VII. HISTORICAL

XVIII. THE STORY OF THE HAT 172

    Men's Hats—Women's Hats—Significance of Headdress

Glossary 185
References 188
The Index 189

LIST OF ILLUSTRATIONS

Shepherdess —Empress Eugénie . . . . *Frontispiece*

	PAGE
1. Color chart	6
2. Measuring diameter of brim	11
3. Two diameters of headsize	11
4. Cutting patterns	12
5. Pattern for brim	13
6. Cutting headsize (Method 1)	14
7. Cutting headsize (Method 3)	15
8. Variations of brim (Method 3)	15
9. Straight-brim pattern	16
10. Drooping or upturning brim	17
11. Irregular-shaped brim	17
12. Cutting brim from material	18
13. Paper mold	20
14. Curved side band	22
15. Joining tip and side band	23
16. Sectional crown	24
17. Materials for frames	27
18. Tommy iron	29
19. Pliers	29
20. Wooden crown mold	30
21. Braids, types	33
22. Tagal plaque	35
23. Tuscan, Swiss hair, and visca	36
24. Comparison of inches and lignes	39
25. Wiring headsize	44
26. Bracing headsize	44
27. Binding edge of brim	45
28. Free-hand molding	47
29. Crown mold (buckram wired)	49
30. Molding crown of crinoline	50
31. Band with stiff tip	51
32. Band with soft tip	52
33. Joining headsize wire	56
34. Attaching spoke wires to headsize wires	57
35. Wire frame, slashed	61
36. Wire frame prepared for molding	64
37. Molding willow over wire frame	65
38. Willow frame removed from mold	65
39. Molding over paper frame	66
40. Construction of wire crown	67

LIST OF ILLUSTRATIONS

41. Wire crown, mold	67
42. Stretching material on frame	73
43. Finishing edge of brim	75
44. Covering tip	79
45. Joining side band and tip	80
46. Plain side band and full and plain tip	81
47. Molding braid brim over wire frame	85
48. Molding braid crown over wire frame	87
49. Backstitch	91
50. Catch stitch	91
51. Catstitch	92
52. Simulated fold	92
53. Slip stitch	93
54. Tie tack	93
55. Wire stitch	94
56. Cutting bias	96
57. Joining bias fold	96
58. Flat fold	97
59. Milliner's fold	98
60. Bias fold extending from brim	101
61. Covering top of brim	101
62. Sectional facing	103
63. Covering cord	104
64. Covering cord, wire inside	105
65. Brim of bias folds and braid	108
66. Crown of bias folds	109
67. Brim made with ribbon and yarn	111
68. Shirred hat	114
69. Stitched or hemstitched brim	115
70. Tam	121
71. Ribbon bows	126
72. Frames for bows	127
73. Ribbon bows	129
74. Plaitings on wired foundation	130
75. Ribbon cockades	131
76. Methods 1 and 2 for making cockade	132
77. Method 3 for making cockade	132
78. Variations of ribbon cockade and tailored bow	133
79. Pattern for large flowers	134
80. Novelty trimmings	*facing* 134
81. Making velvet flowers	139
82. Making silk flowers	140
83. Futurist rose, process	140
84. Futurist rose, finished	141
85. Poppy pattern	142
86. Poppy, center	143
87. Detail for daisy petal	144
88. Tailored rose	144

LIST OF ILLUSTRATIONS

89.	Bell flower, stamens	146
90.	Bell flower	147
91.	Leaf and bud for bell flower	148
92.	Bud and tendril	148
93.	Georgette petals	149
94.	Wire frame for petals	149
95.	Organdy flower	150
96.	Yarn flower No. 1	151
97.	Yarn flower No. 2	151
98.	Yarn trimmings	153
99.	Straw trimmings	154
100.	Quill foundation	155
101.	Blanket stitch	156
102.	Chain stitch	157
103.	Couching stitch	157
104.	Cross-stitch	157
105.	Darning stitch	157
106.	French knots	158
107.	Knot stitch	158
108.	Lazy-daisy stitch	158
109.	Leaf stitch	158
110.	Outline stitch	159
111.	Satin stitch	159
112.	Seed stitch	159
113.	Petasus	173
114.	Francis I	174
115.	Charles XIII of France	175
116.	The Slouched Hat	175
117.	Napoleon	176
118.	Puritan hat	177
119.	Egyptian headdress	178
120.	Hennin	178
121.	Anne of Brittany	179
122.	Mary, Queen of Scots	179
123.	Eighteenth-century headdress	180
124.	Poke bonnet	181
125.	Dutch cap	183

THE PREFACE

The material presented here on the choice and the making of hats has been accumulated during many years of teaching and shop practice. All methods given are those which have proved successful. Throughout the book emphasis is placed upon the need for studying the mode and adapting it to the individual. Repeated suggestions are made for modification of the hats and trimmings herein described.

Millinery is an art based upon enduring principles of design. Therefore this phase of the subject has been given considerable space. The relation of the hat to the mode of hairdress and its place in the entire costume is a design problem.

The importance of art principles which underly the choice of a hat is expressed by a leading representative of the industry: "Our experience in supplying hats to this and adjacent countries leads us to believe that the development of the *artistic sense* as applied to women's wearing apparel is a subject whose importance is not fully realized."

Because of the frequent changes in hairdress and hats, and in the manner of wearing the hat, it has seemed advisable to omit present-day models. Therefore portions of hats and details of construction only are given.

The place of the hat in history has been reviewed, to give a sense of perspective. This review shows that something permanent has come down through the centuries. Types of hats reappear from time to time in modified form.

The book is offered as a text for millinery classes in trade schools, high schools, normal schools, and universities. It should prove valuable also to the home demonstration agent, to the homemaker, to the apprentice in the shop, and to all others interested in making or buying of hats.

Grateful acknowledgment is expressed to the following, who have given valuable assistance in the preparation of the manuscript: Professor Effie I. Raitt; Associate Professor Grace G. Denny, Department of Home Economics; Miss Harriet Westmoreland, editorial secretary (all of the University of Washington); Mrs. Bertha L. Aldous, formerly instructor in Pratt Institute; and De-Clercq-Wirth & Company, wholesale milliners, Seattle, Washington. To Gage Brothers & Company, Chicago, designers and manufacturers of the Gage hat and importers of millinery novelties (a portion of whose letter is quoted above), is due warm appreciation for their reading and helpful criticism of the manuscript.

HATS
AND HOW TO MAKE THEM

PART I. CHARACTER IN A HAT

CHAPTER I

THE CHOICE OF A HAT

SELECTION OFTEN DIFFICULT: Cost Limits Choice—Observe Contour and Coloring—How to Wear the Hat

TEST OF A BECOMING HAT: Importance of Outline

COLOR AND TEXTURE: Color—Advantage of Color Terms—Use of the Color Chart—Effect of Artificial Light—Texture

Every woman would like a definite formula for choosing a becoming hat. It would be easy enough to walk into a shop and buy one if the same rule could be applied universally.

Small wonder the shopper is overwhelmed as she finds each season the shapes radically changed and the colors unfamiliar. The charm of millinery owes its secret to the element of surprise. However much the popular mind may rebel against the thraldom of fashion, it is a stupendous force which cannot be diverted. The importer of millinery goods in Dorothy Canfield Fisher's story "Hats" is made to say, "Style is one of the great obscure mysteries of life."

There are some fortunate women who seem made for milliners' models. Such a woman can try on a sailor, cloche, or turban, a large hat, an inexpensive, or an exclusive one, with almost equal success. However, this is not true of the majority of women. The salesgirl is called upon to use all her skill in finding a hat that will bring out her customer's best features.

SELECTION OFTEN DIFFICULT

There is no woman who cannot be improved by "just the right hat." If she is fatigued or in ill health, she requires all the more care in fitting a hat to her face. If she feels well dressed and her friends take pleasure in her hats, she will return to the milliner who successfully diagnosed her case.

It is not always possible to get the appropriate hat for the person. Lack of judgment, want of a discriminating milliner, and financial limitations often hamper the woman who would be well dressed.

Hats are designed to suit the prevailing mode in hairdress. When ear puffs are worn, the crowns are large; when the huge pompadour is in style, the hat is of necessity placed high on the head. Likewise the general contour of the hat is in harmony with the fashionable neck line of the dress. In the sixteenth century, during the time of Catherine de Medici, the high neck was in vogue and the hair was piled on top of the head. To complete this silhouette a tiny bonnet was worn. Later the flat Van Dyck collar brought the hair down on the neck and the hat became larger.

The woman who disregards entirely the mode in hairdressing will always experience difficulty in finding a becoming hat. This does not mean that everyone should follow the fashion in hair arrangement. It merely explains one of the common trials of hat hunting.

There is a general belief among women that men, because of their conventional hair cut and the apparent standardized style of hats, have no difficulty in choosing a hat. A visit to the haberdasher's will dispel this idea. Men find many subtle differences in the height of crown, width and turn of brim, details of band, binding, and color, which cause them to hesitate long before making the final selection.

While money is an important factor in the choice of a hat, a woman of good taste can frequently complete her costume with a low-priced though suitable and becoming model. One lacking taste would accomplish less with more money. If a woman has unlimited means, the problem need not be great, for she can place herself in the hands of an expert. There are artists in hat designing who make a study of each customer and create a model uniquely suited to her personality.

Cost limits choice. The average woman does not have this freedom. She usually estimates a sum for the family hat bill. Hats beyond this price level cannot be considered. If this allowance permits only one hat each season, there is all the greater need for discriminating choice. It is better to err on the side of plainness than overelaborateness. A street hat may not appear out of place at a tea or luncheon, but a picture hat, appropriate at formal functions, is grotesque when worn on a marketing trip.

Observe contour and coloring. If the customer is young and observes the prevailing mode of hairdressing, she will find many hats suited to her face. While a beautiful face is an asset, no one need be discouraged because of irregular features. Every person has one or more redeeming points. It may be hair, skin, or eyes. The discriminating woman will learn to "play up" her good points, which will leave the unfortunate ones blurred.

There are, to be sure, the usual types of faces: the long thin face, the round face, the face with receding chin or prominent nose. It would be simple enough to recommend the general shape of hat for each face if the head, neck, and shoulders as well conformed to type. However, the round face goes with sloping shoulders just as often as with square ones. The receding chin may accompany the long thin neck or the short plump one.

The coloring of skin, hair, and eyes will differ; likewise, the age of the face. Neither do the size and proportions of the entire figure always correspond to the type of face. All these factors are to be reckoned with, and will shed light upon the perplexing search for a hat.

How to wear the hat. Fashion decrees each season how the hat shall be placed on the head. To ignore this custom makes a woman appear out of date. If, for example, the mode calls for large crowns fitting closely over the hair and placed level with the eyebrows, these hats are built with certain definite proportions. When such a hat is placed high upon the forehead or tilted at an angle, it is thrown out of line.

TEST OF A BECOMING HAT

The well-chosen hat is not seen as a distinct feature, but becomes a part of the person. It merely completes the costume as a whole. In other words, it is a frame for the face, which, after all, should be the center of interest. The outline of head and hair should be closely related to that of the hat. It is usually necessary to try several shapes, observing the different silhouettes made by the shoulders, head, and hat. The becomingness of the rear and side views of the hat is quite as important as the front, because the wearer is seen from all sides.

The final decision, however, should be based upon the outline of the entire figure. A hat chosen before a small mirror is likely to be disappointing when the woman sees herself at full length. An extremely large hat can be worn to better advantage with a long skirt than with a short one. In fact, Fashion usually takes care of these matters and provides long skirts at the same time that she offers large hats. Actresses who study the art of dressing sometimes make use of this principle and appear in a gown with a train or with a fur scarf over the arm to balance a large hat. It will be observed also that solid materials like velvet make a hat look larger than does transparent material. In other words, if there are two hats of the same size, one made of maline and the other of velvet, the latter will appear larger.

Importance of outline. The apparent height of a tall woman may be lessened or the stature of a short one may be increased by the careful choice of a hat. This is largely a matter of experiment when one is trying the hats. There is a popular notion that the tall woman should always wear a drooping brim. This statement in itself is not entirely correct, because features as well as height determine the kind of hat to be worn. The drooping brim tends to accentuate the long curved nose or the retroussé nose. The owner of the Roman nose may wear an upturning brim. A flat brim with a straight or irregular edge makes the short upturning nose less obvious. In general, angular features are not so pronounced when round brims and soft edges such as ostrich or plaitings are used. The very round face is seldom improved by a round rolling brim.

COLOR AND TEXTURE

While the matter of proportion and line is fundamental in hat designing, color and texture are next in importance. The observer seldom analyzes a hat to know why it is good. She feels satisfied with the result, but she may not know how much of her pleasure is due to a successful combination of colors and materials.

Color. A thoroughly pleasing color effect is achieved only when the hat is in harmony with the complexion of the wearer. Her coloring is usually spoken of in terms of hair and eyes. The blue-eyed woman is supposed to wear blue gracefully. Whether she can or not depends almost entirely upon the color of her skin. In other words, we cannot generalize about the gray-haired or red-haired woman or the brown-eyed woman. There are as many types of skin as there are of hair and eyes. Complexions cannot be easily classified. The so-called blond type may cover an example of clear skin, the florid face, or one of yellowish cast. In fact, all skins are more or less yellow. We are not a *white* race. Every skin contains considerable color, and yellow is the one that predominates.

In order to understand what colors may be used for hats it is necessary to examine color and observe the phenomena of color harmonies.

The greatest natural spectacle of color is the rainbow. In it are found all the known colors. This phenomenon is explained by the fact that the sun's rays passing through the raindrops are broken into their elements of color and appear as the rainbow band. Strange as it may seem, white light is made up of the colors of the rainbow, and black is the absence of color.

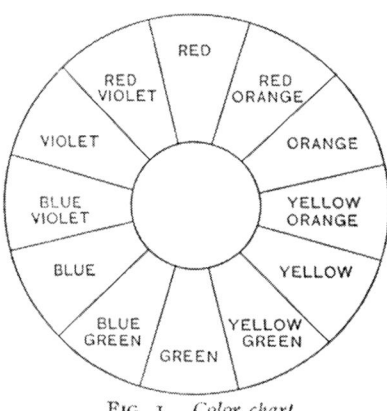

Fig. 1. *Color chart*

It is possible to reproduce rainbow colors by using an instrument called the spectroscope. It separates white light into what is known as the spectrum band. Here, as in the rainbow, the colors blend into one another. Red passes from red orange to orange, and yellow orange to yellow, and so on. At one side of the band appears red and at the other red violet. If these are placed side by side, the color wheel shown in Fig. 1 is the result. Such a chart is useful for explaining combinations of color. It will be observed that the colors on one side of the circle produce a different feeling in the beholder from those on the opposite side. For instance, red, orange, yellow, and yellow green seem cheerful and light-producing. They are spoken of as *warm colors*. Likewise those opposite—green, blue green, blue, blue violet, and violet—are referred to as *cool colors*. They are the retreating colors.

Advantage of color terms. In speaking of color it is convenient to use the terms by which color properties are defined. The darkness or lightness of a color is called its *value*. Its brightness or dullness or purity is *intensity* or *chroma*. The color itself, as, for instance, red distinguished from yellow red or bluish red, is known as *hue*. Every color has these three dimensions, or *constants*, as they are sometimes called.

It is impossible to think of a red rose without picturing a red of certain purity or brightness and of certain darkness or lightness. Light values are usually called *tints*. Pink is a tint of red. Rose is a tint of red, but the kind of rose (whether a bluish rose or a yellowish rose) means the hue. The rose may be dull or bright, according to its intensity.

Use of the color chart. The reader need not be disturbed by the apparent conflicts in color theory in books. The scientific explanation of color takes account only of colored light. The charts shown in most texts represent the colors from the standpoint of the artist who is working with pigments. Such a chart appears on page 6. This explanation is the one commonly used and is simple to understand, since the circle may be easily divided into three parts to show the three primary hues—red, yellow, and blue. When paints or dyes are pure, these hues may be mixed as indicated, producing the so-called secondary hues—orange, green, and violet or purple.

It will be observed that those hues lying next to each other on the chart are harmonious. They are colors frequently seen together in nature. For example, in the spring the blue green and green of trees, the yellow-green of new leaves and yellow of blossoms form what is known as a *dominant harmony*.

One of the strangest things that colors do to each other is evident in the effect produced by placing side by side any pair of hues which lie opposite each other on the color chart. Red and green, or blue and orange, or violet and yellow in such relation appear brighter than they do in the spectrum or when placed upon a background of white. These pairs of colors are called *complements*.[1] When red paint or dye is mixed with a

---

[1] The exact complement of red is blue green; of yellow is violet; and of blue is red orange. If the axes on the circle are turned slightly, the correct complements will be in place.
The chart shown is the one that explains the mixing of pigments and not the effect of colored lights.

little green, the red is dulled, grayed, or neutralized. A larger quantity of green will reduce the red until it becomes more and more neutral. Finally a sort of brown will appear.

Most colors used in dress are low in intensity; that is, they have been grayed by the admixture of the complementary hue. Hues of greatest intensity are as a rule used in small areas. A close turban may be made of cerise, but a picture hat needs only a splash of brilliant color.

Complements, as blue and orange, used together at full intensity and in equal quantities are tiresome. If one of the two is reduced in quantity, the effect will be more pleasing. Or, one of the hues may be neutralized or grayed slightly, or two or more intensities of the same hue may be used with its complement. Two brilliant complements may be used together if a third having something in common with the other two is introduced, as a soft green with blue and orange. Likewise a touch of neutral—as black, white, gray, or silver—will relieve the sharp contrast and add to the interest of the composition.

Any hue has the tendency to bring out its complement if the two are placed side by side. This fact should be remembered when a woman with a yellowish skin is tempted to decide upon a blue-violet or lavender hat.

Often the addition of a veil may serve to make the transition between the color of the hat and the face. For example, there are cases where a purple hat is made more becoming by the use of a purple-blue veil.

Effect of artificial light. It might be stated here that some colors undergo a change when placed in artificial light. Yellow rays tend to absorb the yellow in a compound color. For example, orange appears pinkish and green becomes bluer. This difficulty is overcome by the use of a special "daylight" lamp such as will be found in the better department stores and shops.

The matter of choosing color in a hat, therefore, should receive much consideration. The combination of hues in the hat itself should create harmony, but the color composition as a whole must include the color of hair, eyes, and skin.

Texture. Differences in color are more easily perceived than the contrast of surface effects on various materials. For example, velvet, taffeta, and georgette each create a different impression. This quality in fabrics is called *texture*. Each material has a characteristic texture. Some fabrics, as velvet, have a variety of surface effects. A rich Lyons velvet having an erect pile suggests something very different from the velveteen used in a sports hat.

The successful combination of textures requires imagination and judgment. New materials and new combinations appear each season. When georgette was first used with fur, and taffeta with organdy, the result was startling. Gradually the public became accustomed to this unusual treatment of textures. Those who create hat designs are more sensitive to the possibilities of combining textures than the untrained woman.

For a face showing the lines of age or ill health, textures may be chosen which will soften these lines. Velvet, fur, ostrich, or plaitings worn next the face have a flattering effect on the thin or tired woman. Stiff materials, on the other hand, such as metal cloth, lustrous straws, and taffeta, are trying, while the same materials set off a youthful face.

PART II. PAPER PATTERNS

CHAPTER II

HOW TO MAKE PAPER PATTERNS

BRIM COPYING: Measuring Brim—Cutting Brim—Cutting Headsize—Three Methods—Copying

BRIM DESIGNING: Even Brim—Uneven Brim—Slightly Drooping or Upturning Brim—Irregular-Shaped Brim

PAPER BRIM CONSTRUCTION: Cutting Brim—Making Brim—Sewing Band to Headsize—Making Paper Mold

CROWN DESIGNING: Measuring Crowns—Cutting Straight Side Band—Cutting Curved Side Band

PAPER CROWN CONSTRUCTION: Cutting—Joining Tip and Side Band—Joining Plain Band and Gathered Tip—Making Sectional Crown—Making Crown in One Piece—Joining Brim and Crown

Fashioning paper patterns affords excellent practice for beginning the study of hat design. It gives the worker confidence and encourages her to use originality. No expensive material need be wasted while one is learning. Newspaper, tissue, or wrapping paper may be used for developing patterns. Practice with paper patterns also gives the amateur a knowledge of the construction of hats. She sees how easily changes can be made by a slash here, a bend there, or by taking from or adding to brim or crown.

The fundamental thing about a hat is its shape or outline, which assumes different proportions each season. It is the ambition of every designer to catch the spirit of the mode.

BRIM COPYING

Measuring brim. Select your best fitting hat as a basis for measurements. If it does not fit perfectly, change the measurements by adding to or deducting from one of the diameters.

HOW TO MAKE PAPER PATTERNS

A well-fitting headsize is nearly always oval, and this oval varies according to the shape of the head and the manner of

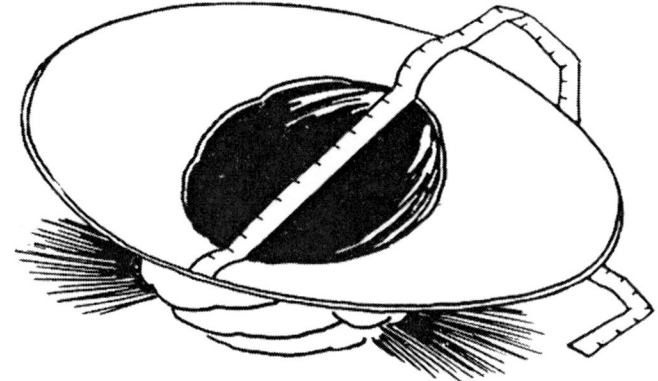

FIG. 2. *Measuring diameter of brim from front to back*

wearing the hair. The headsize measure is one of the most important in hat making. The headsize of the average bobbed head is $19\frac{1}{2}$ to $21\frac{1}{2}$ inches; for others, $22\frac{1}{2}$ to 24 inches. The hat should fit rather snugly at the sides, but may fit loosely from front to back, for pressure on the forehead makes the wearer uncomfortable.

After choosing a hat that fits the head well, measure as follows for brim and headsize. (Work out a problem as you read and the directions will be easily understood.)

1. On underside of hat place tape measure on center back at outer edge of brim and let tapeline follow the line of hat to headsize, across headsize, then to edge of brim at center front.

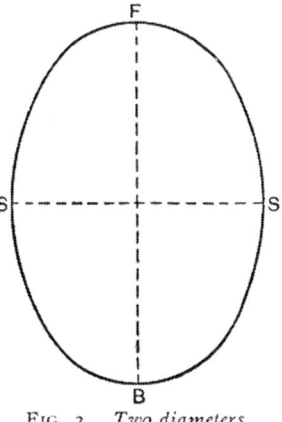

FIG. 3. *Two diameters of headsize*

2. Measure from side to side in the same way. These measurements must follow the shape of the hat or it will be too small. Do not take a short cut across a drooping brim, but place the tape measure easily in the curves (Figs. 2 and 3).

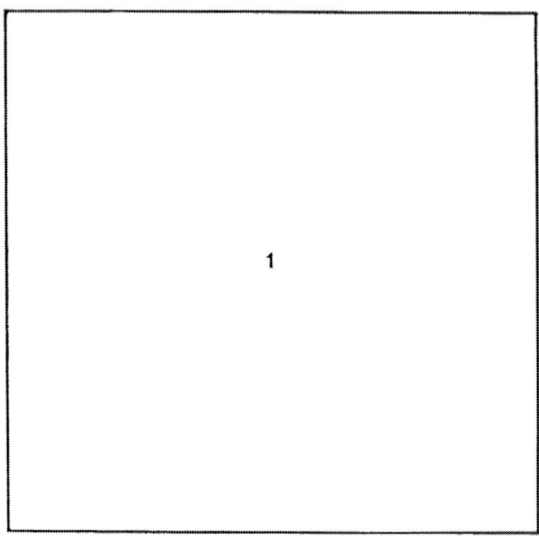
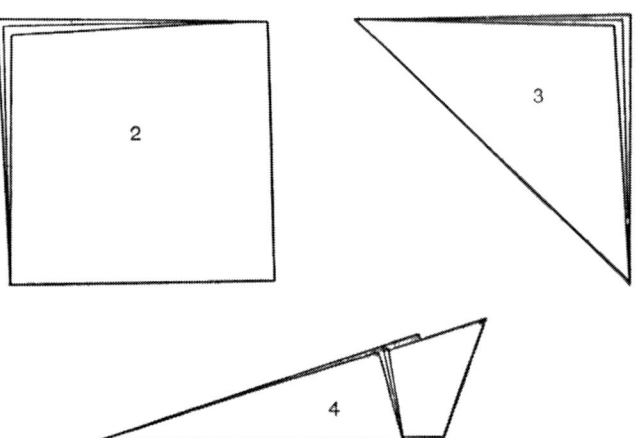

FIG. 4. *Cutting patterns.* (1) Square of paper the diameter of brim; (2) square folded in quarters; (3) square folded forming a triangle; (4) fold triangle twice

HOW TO MAKE PAPER PATTERNS

3. Measure headsize from back to front for the longer diameter and from side to side for the shorter diameter.

Cutting brim. Cut a square of paper equal to the greater diameter of the brim, fold this square in halves, then in halves again, making it measure one-fourth of the large square which has two folded sides and two cut sides. Hold center of large square in left hand and fold again so that folded sides fall together forming a triangle. This triangle must be folded twice more with the shortest side of cut edge on top. Be sure to keep the point well defined (Fig. 4).

Measure from the point, along folded edges of triangle, a distance equal to one-half the longer diameter of brim

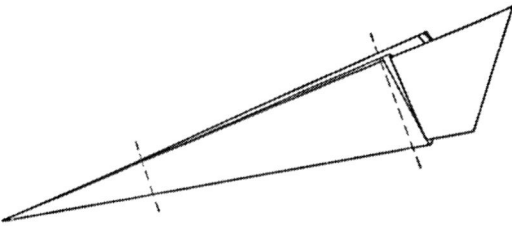

FIG. 5. *Pattern for brim. Cut on dotted lines for circle and headsize*

measurement. Cut straight across at this point (Fig. 5). This cutting must be accurate to prevent the completed circle from having scallops or points. The circle forms the outer edge of the brim. Do not unfold until headsize is cut.

To measure actual headsize, place a tape around the head at the place where the hat is worn customarily. This measurement should be taken comfortably close but not tight. Allowance for making is always added to headsize measurement.

Cutting headsize. There are several ways of cutting the headsize. Three methods are given here:

Method No. 1. Measure from point along folded edges of triangles a distance equal to one-half the shorter diameter of the headsize. Cut straight across to form a circle. The result of the second cutting will give two circles, the outer one being the edge of the brim and the inner one the headsize, which must be changed into an oval.

Unfold the circle until it is in quarters (Fig. 6). This will give two single folds and one double fold. Mark "front" on one and "back" on the other single fold. Mark the double fold the "sides." Use one-half the difference between the two diameters of the headsize and measure this distance from the inner circle, on the single fold. For example, if the diameters of the headsize are 8 by 6, the difference is 2 inches. Use one-half the difference (1 inch) in altering circle to form oval. This gives a plain flat sailor brim which may be used as a foundation for other shapes.

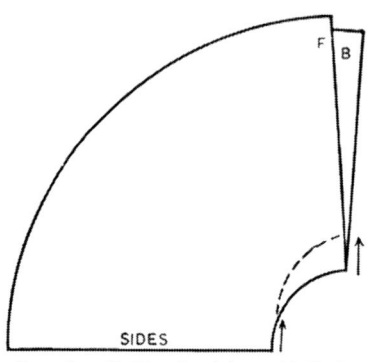

FIG. 6. *Cutting headsize—Method 1*

1. On fold marked "front" measure 1 inch from inner circle.
2. On inner circle measure 1 inch from fold marked "side."
3. Connect these two points with a gradual curve and cut.

Method No. 2. Before unfolding the circle measure the head where the hat is to be worn. From center of circle measure toward edge one-sixth of headsize desired (tight measurement). At this point cut straight across, forming a circle. Open circle and change inner circle to oval as directed under Method No. 1. Fold in quarters and mark on center-front fold 1 inch from inner circle; and on inner circle mark 1 inch from side. Connect the two points with a gradual curve and cut on this line. This gives the desired shape and the extra size that will be taken up in making.

Method No. 3. Use measurements in Method No. 1 (8 inches by 6 inches). Cut pattern for headsize as follows: Measure and cut a square equal to the greater diameter and form a circle. Fold in quarters. Measure down and mark on fold *from* edge one-half the difference between the two diameters (1 inch).

HOW TO MAKE PAPER PATTERNS

On the opposite fold measure on the edge from the fold (Fig. 7) 1 inch. Connect the two points thus formed by a gradual curve and cut on this line. Open the oval, cut pattern from a piece of cardboard or stiff paper, and place at any point on the circle cut for brim. Mark around with pencil and cut. If the headsize is drawn on different parts of the frame, a variety of shapes may be made (Fig. 8). This method of cutting the headsize is suitable for the beginner or for a class of children.

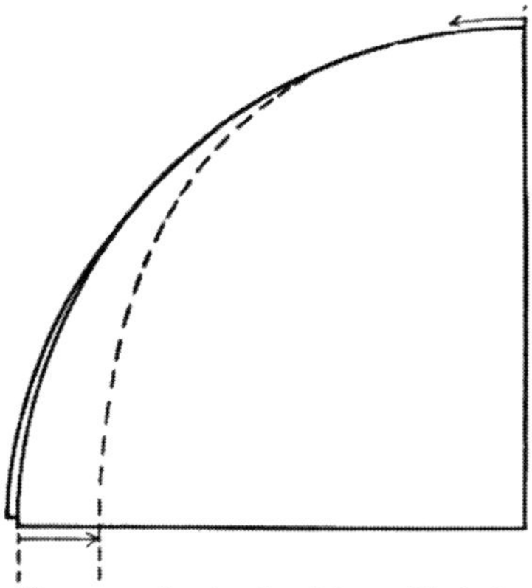

Copying. Measure across the largest diameter of hat brim from underside, add 1 inch, and cut a circle as directed for making patterns. Pin this pattern to underside of brim and at intervals pin plaits in the pattern until it fits brim perfectly. Trim close to outer edge. Cut headsize following lines of brim. Before removing pattern from frame mark carefully front, back, right, and left sides. This pattern cannot always be cut flat from the material without a seam. The seam must come at back or where the trimmings will hide it. Cut pattern open from edge to headsize. Make allowance for seams later when cutting out materials.

FIG. 7. *Cutting headsize — Method 3*

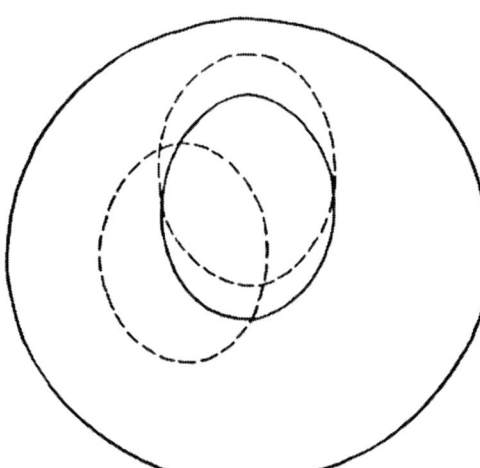

FIG. 8. *Variations of brim with changing position of headsize — Method 3*

HATS AND HOW TO MAKE THEM

BRIM DESIGNING

The size of a brim is often deceptive. If the brim curves upward or downward, it appears smaller than a straight brim or sailor. To estimate width of brim, measure from the headsize out on the underside of brim.

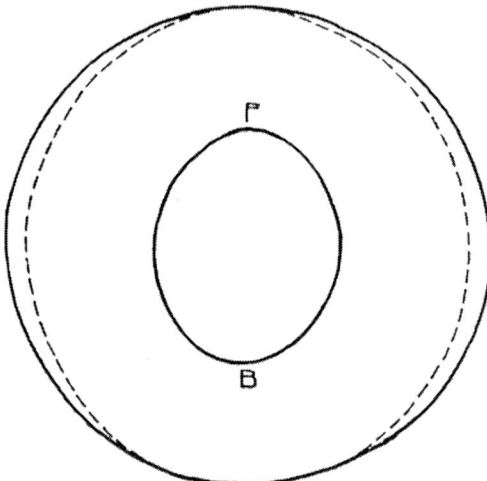

FIG. 9. *Straight-brim pattern broader at sides; even brim—dotted lines*

Crowns vary widely in style and sometimes tend to make the brims appear smaller than they really are. Trimmings are also likely to make the hat appear smaller.

Even brim. If an even brim all around is desired, fold the paper in quarters as directed for cutting the first brim (see page 13). On single folds measure 1 inch from edge of brim. From double folds measure 1 inch on outer circle. Connect the two points with a gradual curve. Great care is necessary in making this curve to avoid points; however, some designs require points or squares. Experiment freely with designs when using practice material. It is important to have a clear conception of the design.

Uneven brim. Cut a square and form a circle as directed for the first brim, but do not cut headsize. Open circle and refold so that one side projects beyond the other. Consider the prevailing mode in deciding proportions. There may be a difference of from 2 to 4 inches or more in the two sides. The wider part may be used for front, back, or side. Fold in quarters and cut headsize as directed for Method No. 1 or 2, or cut a circle and experiment with headsize as shown in Fig. 8.

Mark pattern front, back, right, and left sides. These markings are important if the oval headsize has been cut in the pattern.

Slightly drooping or upturning brim. Cut the pattern through center back. Pin $\frac{1}{4}$-inch dart in center front on edge of circle and graduate to headsize, which should not be made smaller. (This removes $\frac{1}{2}$ inch.) On each side of center back make fold $\frac{1}{4}$ inch at outer edge, graduating to a point at headsize. Take care not to reduce headsize. Keep pattern on the table so that darts

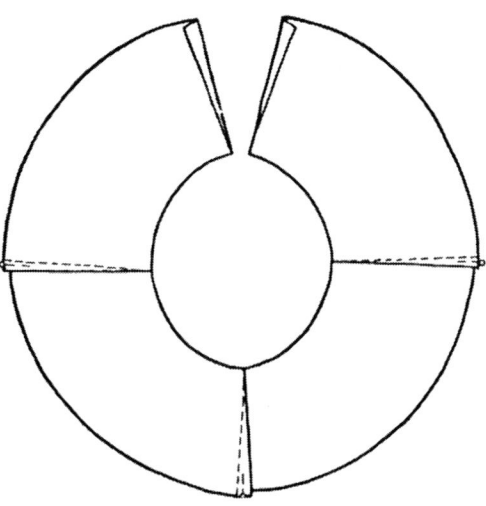

FIG. 10. *Slightly drooping or upturning brim*

may be adjusted easily. If a greater droop is desired, make plaits at quarters and eighths or sixteenths, etc. Remember that each $\frac{1}{4}$-inch plait removes $\frac{1}{2}$ inch from edge of brim. Hence this is causing brim to change more and more from the original straight brim to one that curves downward or rolls upward (Fig. 10).

For the regular-shaped brim the pattern must be

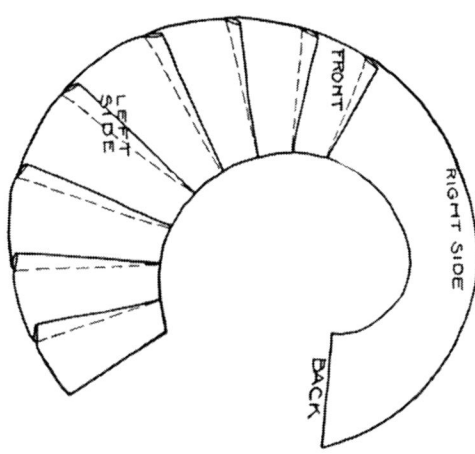

FIG. 11. *Darts laid in pattern to give irregular-shaped brim*

darted evenly all around with equal darts and regular spacings.

Irregular-shaped brim. Fashion requires occasionally an irregular brim wide at front, side, or back with an abrupt turn. The wide side can be made to have an extreme turn by darts or plaits placed all on one side. This extreme turn can be made with about eight plaits (Fig. 11, page 17). Remember to keep the divisions equal. As the pattern was cut without plaits, the opposite or narrow side may be left unaltered. The result is a narrow side which stands almost straight out from the head.

It is advisable to practice making hats of paper, placing the plaits at irregular intervals and comparing with the hat made with plaits at regular intervals.

PAPER BRIM CONSTRUCTION

It is not necessary for the beginner to waste valuable material in experimenting with shapes. She may cut the pattern from heavy paper (preferably wrapping paper) and pin or sew it together. Newspaper may be used, especially if two or three layers are pinned together. The paper hat may be tried on and altered before the design is put in permanent form.

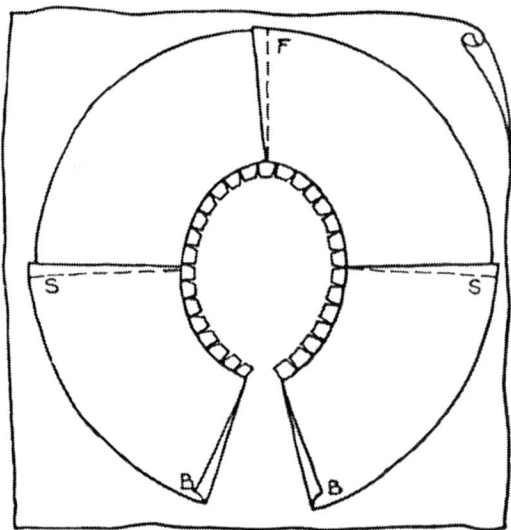

FIG. 12. *Cutting brim from paper or other materials*

Cutting brim. Pin pattern to paper or material. If pattern is approximately the correct size, cut the material following edge of brim. If plaits have been taken in the brim to remove some of the fullness, a seam in the back will be necessary. Outline pattern with pencil or chalk, on each side of back and at headsize. Allow ½ inch on each side of back for seam. At headsize allow ¾ inch. Cut material on these lines. Then slash straight in from the ¾-inch marking to original headsize, making slashes 1 inch apart (Fig. 12). These little slashed pieces must be turned up at right angles to the brim. They furnish a foundation for strengthening the brim and for adjusting the crown.

Making brim. Overlap edges at the back, pin, and sew them together. Cut a straight piece of paper 1½ inches wide. The length must be the circumference of the headsize plus 1 inch for making and 2 inches for overlapping. Fold width through middle, making a double strip ¾ inch wide. Pin ends together, overlapping them 2 inches. Place joining at back against the ¾-inch slashed pieces; pin first from back to front, then from side to side. If the headsize is too small, cut the little slashed pieces deeper in the front and back than on the sides. Take care to keep the headsize an oval shape. As stated before, the hat may fit snugly at the sides, but it must be loose from front to back. In fact, the headsize will seem too large now because of the allowance for making.

Sewing band to headsize. With stab stitch sew through and back again, fastening the little slashed pieces firmly to the band. Take stitches just short enough to hold securely in place. If the hat is to be soft when finished, attach this band with running stitch instead of stab stitch. See stab stitch, page 93.

Making paper mold. It is possible to use stiff paper as a mold over which to stretch moistened buckram, willow, flexible or rice net.

Paper molds are satisfactory because they are easily made, are inexpensive, and can be altered on the head to suit individual taste.

Cut an 18-inch square of stiff wrapping paper, express, or butcher's paper. Outline headsize from oval described on page 15. Measure in on this true headsize 1 inch all around, forming an oval 2 inches smaller in diameter. Cut out this oval and slash margin to true headsize. Slashes should be about $\frac{1}{2}$ inch apart.

Bend these slashed pieces up at right angles to the paper. Pin to them a strip of paper 2 inches wide folded in the middle lengthwise and adjusted so as to cover both sides of the slashes. Measure out from headsize the desired width for brim. This brim may be altered to form a drooping or upturning shape or a variation of either by slashes in the brim. Slash from edge to headsize, or only part way, four or eight equal divisions. Overlap the slashes from $\frac{1}{8}$ to $\frac{1}{4}$ inch. If a deeper roll is desired slash at more places. Stay the slashes on the underside of brim with 1-inch strips of stiff paper, pinning on both sides of the outer and inner edges of slashes. The frame shown in Fig. 13 has a brim 3 inches wide slashed halfway in at sixteen equal points.

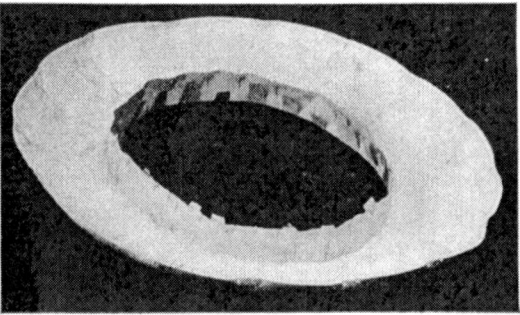

FIG. 13. *Paper mold*

For a brim rolling on one side only, slash and lap on the rolled side. For the straight brim with a 1-inch edge turned up all around, slash in $1\frac{1}{2}$ inches from edge of brim; lap and stay to form amount of roll desired.

The stiff paper mold should be tried on, and alterations in it should be made to suit the wearer before the material is molded over it.

The tissue or newspaper brim pattern given in Fig. 8, page 15, may be used for cutting stiff paper. This method gives the entire outline of the brim, but it must be remembered that the headsize is to be cut 1 inch smaller all around and slashed as in the preceding method.

CROWN DESIGNING

A crown that follows somewhat the shape of the head and face is usually most becoming. (See chapter i, "The Choice of a Hat.")

Throughout the centuries crowns have changed more radically than brims. (See chapter xviii, "The Story of the Hat.") The proportion of the crown and the way it sets on the head determine where it belongs in style periods. A hat in the vanishing mode may often be brought to date by a rebuilt crown. The soft draping effects in crowns, when popular, lend themselves very well to remodeling.

The height of the crown is of great importance. The prevailing mode determines how high and how large it shall be. Therefore exact dimensions cannot be given.

The simplest crown for pattern work is the two-piece one with the side band and top or tip. The side band may be made straight or curved. The tip of the crown may be round, oval, or any other desired shape.

The sectional crown offers opportunity for variety in paper patterns. It may be combined with the straight or curved side band.

Measuring crowns. To find the dimensions for the side band, copy the crown of an old hat and use the measurements as a basis. Measure around base of crown and around tip (that is, the division line between tip and band), then height of band, diameter of tip from front to back, and diameter from side to side.

If an old crown is not convenient, measure around head piece on top of brim and add 1 inch to the measurement obtained for a close-fitting crown. All seam allowances should be made on materials, not on patterns.

Cutting straight side band. The crown with a straight side band is the simplest. Make the tip any diameter desired. Cut a square and form a circle or oval. For the band cut a straight piece $3\frac{1}{7}$ times the diameter and desired height.

Cutting curved side band. This crown is sometimes called the bell crown, and has a smaller tip than base. The band may be inverted if desired, making a smaller base than tip.

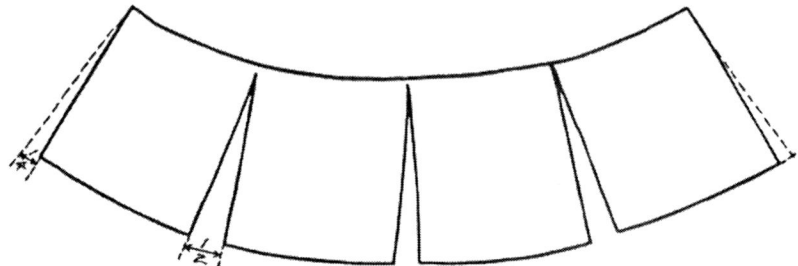

FIG. 14. *Curved side band*

Cut a straight piece of paper equal to the circumference of tip and the desired height. For example, this may be 23 inches long by $3\frac{1}{2}$ inches wide. Fold length of band in halves, then in quarters. Cut on folds of this piece to within $\frac{1}{16}$ inch of opposite side. Place this band on a larger piece of paper. For a slightly curved band spread the three sections $\frac{1}{2}$ inch (Fig. 14). At each end extend the band $\frac{1}{4}$ inch, or half as much as the sections are spread. If a greater curve is desired on this band, it can be obtained by spreading the sections as much as desired. For the tip use headsize pattern, Method 3, page 15.

PAPER CROWN CONSTRUCTION

Cutting. Pin pattern to a piece of stiff paper and cut. At each end allow $\frac{1}{2}$ inch for overlapping.

Joining tip and side band. Stiff paper will not sew in a seam like cloth. Therefore enlarge the tip as follows and attach it to the side band. Pin tip to paper, outline with pencil, and cut $\frac{1}{4}$ inch larger. Slash to original size. Bend down the slashed pieces and sew the side band to them (Fig. 15). In attaching this band to the tip, place the seam at center back. Overlap the band and catch with long stitches.

HOW TO MAKE PAPER PATTERNS

Joining plain band and gathered tip. Crowns are sometimes made with the plain side bands either curved or straight, with full tip. The same tip pattern may be used. It must be enlarged according to the fullness desired for the particular band. For slight fullness on top, the diameter may be 2 inches larger, i. e., 1 inch larger all around. Practice varying this tip pattern and adjusting it to side bands. Try varying the height of the bands and note results. To adjust this full piece for the tip to the band, divide it in halves and quarters. Gather or plait it and sew it in place.

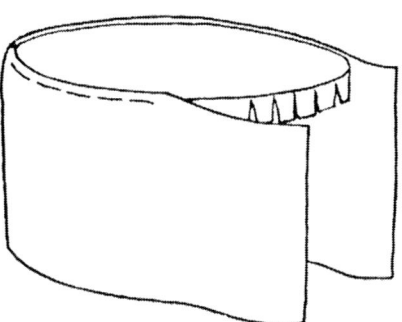

FIG. 15. *Joining tip and side band of stiff paper*

For further practice, try giving the crown added softness as follows: Cut a piece of paper twice the height of the crown and the length of the crown circumference plus overlapping. Fold the paper carelessly around the crown. This takes the place of a bias fold of material or ribbon.

Making sectional crown. Measure from base at back over tip to base in front. Use this dimension for the diameter of the square from which to cut circle.

Open circle and refold in quarters. Draw a line through center of quarters from center of circle to edge of curve, dividing quarter in halves, and large circle in eighths. Measure from both sides of this line on bottom curve one-eighth of the size desired for base of crown. Connect these two points with center of circle by a gradual outward curve (Fig. 16, page 24). A little practice will train the worker in making these curves. A variety of sectional crowns may be developed by this method.

For a crown in five sections, work with the circle spread out on the table, then design sections from the edge to center. No seams are allowed on these pieces. When cutting from paper for practice, or from material, allow from $\frac{1}{4}$ to $\frac{1}{2}$ inch all around for seams. Pin and baste to get the effect. To obtain the best results in adjusting the crown to the brim, place one section on center front of hat. The seams may be finished with a cord or a binding, or left plain.

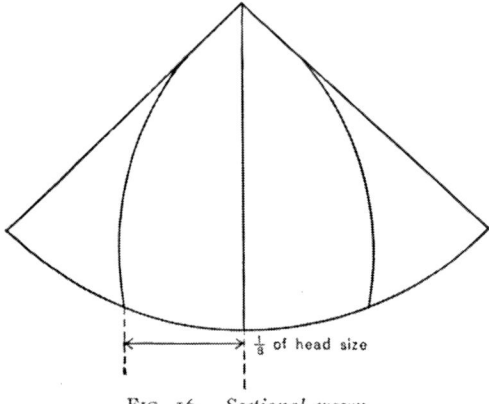

FIG. 16. *Sectional crown*

Another method of making sectional crowns is as follows: Measure from tip of crown to base. Measure the circumference of crown at base. Divide the circumference into 4, 5, or 6 sections, depending upon the number desired; i. e., a crown of 24-inch circumference divided into six sections will make each section 4 inches (not including seams). From tip to base measures 8 inches, making a rectangular piece 4 by 8 inches. For cutting see Fig. 16.

Making crown in one piece. Measure as directed for sectional crown, i. e., height of crown at back, across tip, and height of crown in front. Cut a square and form a circle. This piece is sometimes more effective in an oval instead of a perfect circle. It may be gathered and sewed on a band before being adjusted to the brim, or gathered and placed directly on the brim. Sometimes buttonholes are put around this piece on children's wash hats so that it may be buttoned to the brim.

Joining brim and crown. Pin the crown and the brim together, having seams at center back. Fasten with long stitches.

Stand before a mirror and observe the becomingness of the paper hat. Do not hesitate to bend the brim at any angle, studying all the time the different effects. Sometimes it will be necessary to make the brim smaller by trimming the edges at different places. Again, it may be advisable to add more to the edge of the brim, making the hat larger. At times, it is necessary to slash the brim from edge to headsize, overlapping to remove fullness from certain parts of the hat. Or, slash the brim and set in little pieces if a straight brim is desired. In slashing the brim to add more fullness, be sure to slash through it, i. e., from edge to headsize. Otherwise, the attempt to overlap and to remove fullness will cause little bumps in the pattern at the ends of the darts and the resulting pattern will be unsatisfactory. A carefully developed pattern is essential to successful hat making.

PART III. EQUIPMENT AND MATERIALS

CHAPTER III

EQUIPMENT

EQUIPMENT: Bandeaux—Buckram—Cable Cord—Candle Wicking—Cape Net—Clamps—Crinoline—Device for Steaming—Duck Cloth—Flexible or Elastic Net or J. C. Cloth (Jockey Club)—Glue or Cement—Hat Dye—Hat Lacquer—Panama Cloth—Paper—Rice Net—Tarlatan—Tommy Iron—Tools—Willow—Wire—Wooden Molds

Bandeaux. May be bought ready-made or made at home. Vary in shape and size. Made of buckram or elastic net and covered with velvet.

Buckram. A two-ply fabric stiffened with sizing or glue. Made of crinoline on one side and a coarse, open material on the other. Used for stiff brims and crowns. Black or white. Sold by the yard or in 18-yard bolts. Width, 27 inches.

Cable cord. Black and white. Two sizes, No. 2 and No. 4. Two varieties. One contains no wire, but is merely a wrapped cotton cord. The other contains yarn and fine wire, and is covered with cotton casing. Used as a cord for shirrings, and also as braces in pliable brims. May be used for edge of brims or for finishing crowns or to make corded effects.

Candle wicking. Soft cotton cord. May be used as cable cord.

Cape net. An open, stiff fabric having a square mesh, the same as rice net. Resembles filet net. Heavily sized. It is stiffer than crinoline. Used for crowns and brims. Width, 18 inches and 36 inches.

Clamps. Metal, for connecting ends of wires in making frames. Sizes: No. 1 for lace, No. 2 for frames, No. 3 for steel.

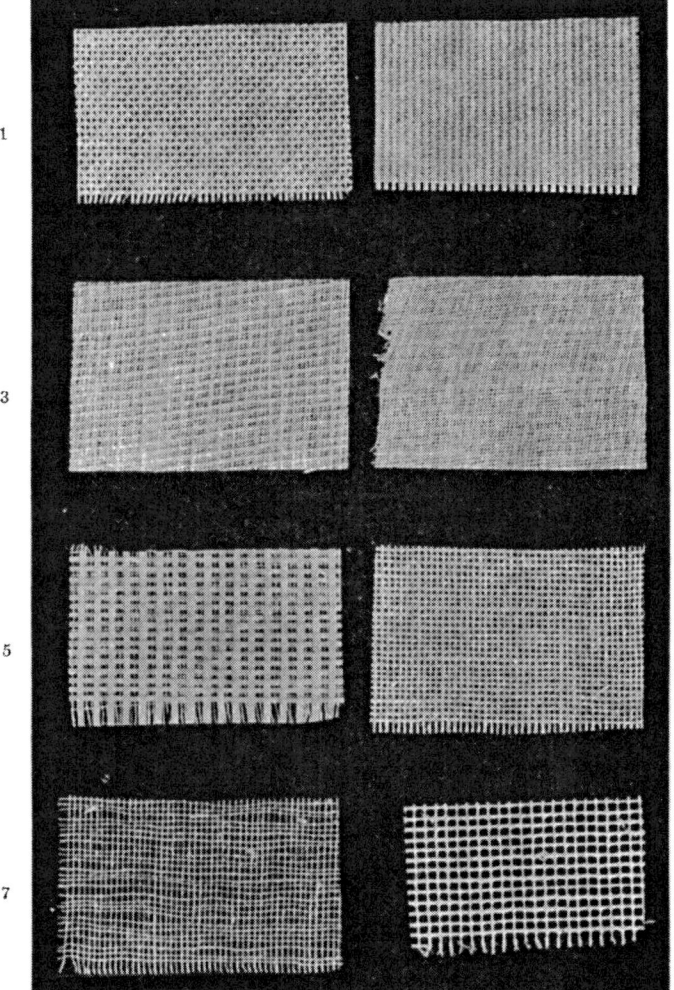

Fig. 17. *Materials for hat frames*

1. Duck cloth
2. Panama
3. Buckram (wrong side)
4. Buckram (right side)
5. Willow (fiber side)
6. Flexible net
7. Crinoline
8. Cape or rice net

Crinoline, two types. (1) A loosely woven, single-ply material. Highly sized with a dull finish. Best known type of crinoline. Used for brims, crowns, and bindings. Comes in 10-yard pieces. White or black. Width, 27 inches. (2) A closely woven, single-ply material, highly sized, very flexible. Excellent for crowns. Used also for brims and bindings. Width, 36 inches.

Device for steaming. A convenient device for steaming can be installed in any classroom or shop where steam is used for heating. The steam line may be tapped at any suitable place for a $\frac{1}{4}$- or $\frac{3}{8}$-inch pipe. Bring the pipe to the desired height and bend it so that the last foot or two is horizontal. The end of the pipe should be above a basin or sink that will catch the condensate. Place an ordinary globe valve at a convenient place in the line to control the steam jet. The job may be done at small cost by any plumber. The same device may be used in a hairdressing establishment. In dressmaking or alteration rooms it is advisable to attach a hose for steaming garments made of pile fabrics.

Duck cloth. A stiff, dull material of rough texture for making hat frames. Difficult to handle. White. Width, 36 inches.

Flexible or elastic net or J. C. cloth (Jockey Club). A loosely woven fabric, pliable and soft, yet with a wiry appearance. Excellent for making soft rolled brims or crowns or placing rolls on edge of brim. Less stiff than duck cloth, but similar. White or maize. Width, 40 inches.

Glue or cement. Comes in quart cans, six-ounce bottles, and six-ounce tubes. Used for gluing fabrics to frames, or wires to ribbon for making bows; for repairing feathers, etc.

Hat dye. For renewing faded straw. Many brands on the market.

Hat lacquer. A sort of varnish for flowers, foliage, hats, etc., to produce shiny effects. Black or white.

Panama cloth. Closely woven cotton fabric similar to flexible net. Wiry and elastic. Color, usually deep cream. May be

EQUIPMENT

used for making the entire hat. Many commercial frames are made of this material. Width, 36 inches.

Paper. Express or butcher's comes in sheets or in rolls; wrapping paper comes in rolls; tissue in sheets.

Rice net. An open, stiff fabric having a square mesh. It resembles filet net. Heavily sized. Used for crowns and brims of hats, especially crowns. White. May be tinted for colored organdy or crêpe hats.

Tarlatan. Thin, very open fabric, square mesh, highly sized and polished. As coarse as thin cheesecloth, very wiry, and transparent. White or colors. Used for interlining crowns, side bands, bows, etc. Width, 54 inches and 60 inches.

FIG. 18. *Tommy iron*

Tommy iron.[1] A patented device (Fig. 18) for pressing small curves in crowns and brims. It is especially desirable for renovating because it may be used in places too small for an ordinary iron.

There are two small ironing heads which may be attached to a handle and used either in an upright position (clamped on the table) or held in the hand like a vacuum cleaner.

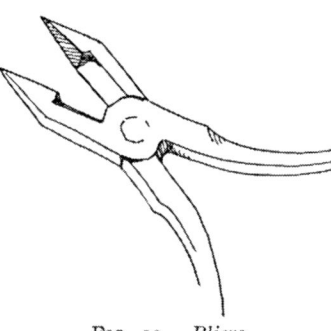

FIG. 19. *Pliers*

One of the iron heads is similar to an iron, but smaller and egg-shaped. The other one is more pointed and has no flat surface. They are heated by electricity.

Tools. Milliner's pliers (Fig. 19) (should have sharp cutting edge, square or pointed end); scissors or shears; razor blade or sharp knife for ripping; pins (box of small pins, and paper of long black-headed pins); thimble; tape

---

[1] The tommy iron is made by Conrad T. Smith, 16 and 18 West 46th Street, New York City.

measure; milliner's needles sizes 2 to 8 (5 to 6 commonly used); milliner's thread (Geneva) (black and white). Any strong luster thread may be used. Sizes 16 to 80 (24 and 30 most popular). Colors in size 30 only.

Willow. A two-ply material made from fine strips of woody fiber woven and pasted to crinoline. There are three grades: one very stiff, one medium stiff, and one without crinoline back. The medium weight is excellent for the beginner. It is more pliable if used with the crinoline side toward the face. Not desirable for crowns. Willow was originally made in Bohemia and Italy, but since the war it has been made in Japan. Sheets, 24 by 36 inches.

FIG. 20. *Wooden hat mold*

Wire. Frame wire Black or white, covered with silk, mercerized cotton, or paper. May be purchased by the bolt or by the yard—stiff, medium, or soft.

Lace wire—same as above, only finer.

Tie wire—different sizes, fine grade the best. Covered as above. Black or white. Usually on spools.

Cable wire—heavy wire covered with silk.

Ribbon wire—flat, covered with cotton. Widths, $\frac{1}{4}$ inch, $\frac{1}{2}$ inch, $\frac{3}{4}$ inch, 1 inch ($\frac{3}{4}$ inch most used). Black or white. Used for wiring bows, edge of brims, and flexible silk hats.

Metal wire—gold and silver. Round wire for making metal hats. Tie wire in same colors.

Steel or spring wire—square or round. Without covering. For sailor frames and hats with cloth brims (halo) having no brim supports or brace wires.

Wooden molds. Wooden molds (Fig. 20, page 30) may be purchased or made to order. A carpenter or manual training teacher can make the block, copying a modern crown. Cedar is the preferred wood, because it may be wetted without cracking.

CHAPTER IV

MATERIALS FOR CONSTRUCTION

BRAIDS: Baby Azure—Belgian Split and China Milan—Birds' Nest—Cellophane—Chenille—Chip—Hair Braid—Hemp—Liséré—Leghorn—Milan—Milan Hemp—Novelties—Panama—Pyroxylin—Tagal—Timbo Braid—Tuscan—Visca—Yedda—Zipper

FABRICS: Beaver Cloth—Broadcloth—Chiffon—Crêpe (Cotton)—Crêpe de Chine—Duvetyn—Faille—Felt—Gingham—Georgette—Grosgrain—Hatter's Plush—Leather—Maline—Messaline—Metal Cloth—Net—Oilcloth—Organdy—Ottoman—Peau de Soie—Ribbons—Satin—Taffeta—Tulle—Veiling—Velvet—Velours

FURS: Beaver—Coney—Ermine—Mink—Mole—Monkey—Seal—Squirrel

BRAIDS

Many hat braids are foreign-made. An increasing number are being produced in this country. Styles in braids are as seasonal as other millinery materials. There are, however, a few standard braids which are found in machine-made hats and which may be purchased by the yard or bolt of ten yards. A plaque is a round flat piece of braid either sewed or woven. It may be made of hemp, yedda, leghorn, or other braids. Following is a list of some common braids used for machine- and hand-made hats.

Baby azure. Made of cotton. It has a dull surface and is used only for machine-made hats and plaques. Comes in black and is of low grade.

Belgian split and China Milan. The two are practically the same and have the same appearance as liséré.

Birds' nest. As the name implies, birds' nest resembles the interlacing of straws. It is very brittle and shiny and is used in blocked hats only.

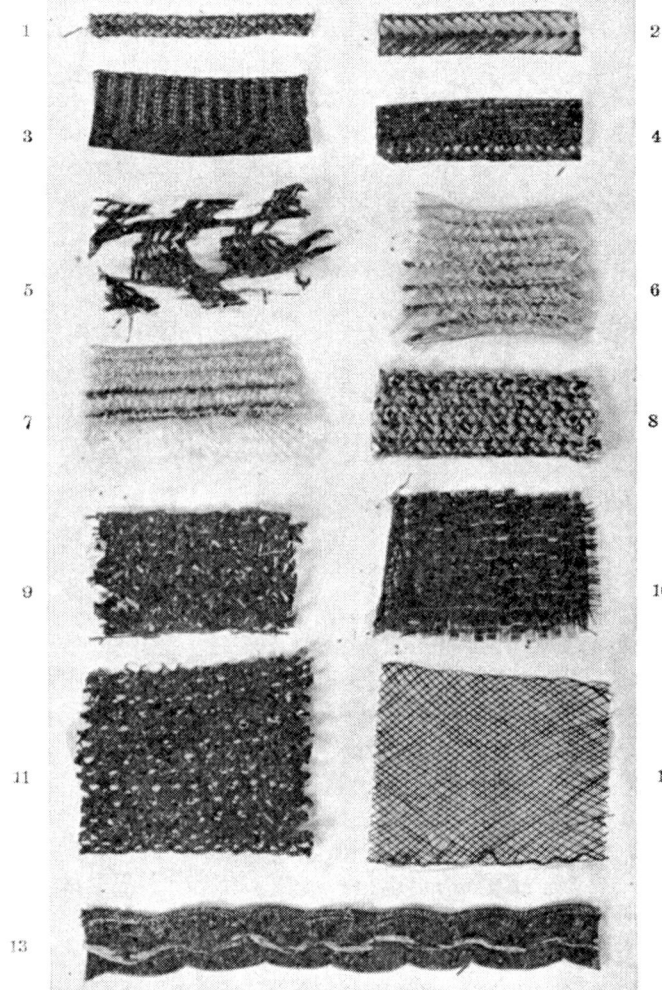

FIG. 21. *Types of braids*

1. Milan hemp
2. Porcupine
3. Silk and felt
4. Liséré
5. Visca and yarn
6. Visca
7. Visca
8. Cellophane and yarn
9. Cellophane and visca
10. Cellophane cloth (bugle cloth)
11. Cellophane (bugle net)
12. Swiss hair
13. Felt and metal

Cellophane. Like visca and pyroxlin, cellophane is a product of the laboratory. It is made in sheets, cut into narrow strips, and combined with other materials for making braids or all-over cloth. Braids and cloth are woven with this composition running through them. It is very lustrous. It looks something like patent leather and comes in all colors.

Chenille. Chenille yarns are woven into chenille braids or combined with any kind of straw or with strips of felt. The chenille cord is used for embroidery.

Chip. A wood fiber. It is the least expensive of braids. In order to make it durable it is paraffined. It is found usually in machine-stitched hats, i. e., not sold by the yard.

Hair braid. As the name suggests, hair braid is made from the manes and tails of horses. It is stiff, dull, and lacy in appearance, and very effective for transparent hats. It is made mostly as braids and plaques, and is manufactured chiefly in Switzerland and somewhat in Germany. It has been largely replaced by manufactured fiber. (See pyroxylin.)

Hemp. Hemp is not a true straw, but is made from fibers of the fleshy leaf of a plant, the abacá or Manila hemp of the Philippines. The finest quality is manufactured in Switzerland; it is also made in Italy, France, and Japan. It is a fine, light-weight, pliable, and strong braid which dyes easily. The braid is about $\frac{1}{8}$ inch wide and must have five or seven, sometimes more, rows joined in order to make a braid of convenient width for handmade hats.

Liséré. This is a very shiny, stiff, brittle, narrow braid. It is made chiefly in Japan and is sewed into hats by machine or by hand. It is also imported from Switzerland, Belgium, and China. The braid by the bolt is made of a series of small strands stitched together in much the same way as hemp braid. Before using this braid place it between dampened newspaper or tissue paper about two hours. This removes the shiny surface. Lacquer the hat to restore the finish.

MATERIALS FOR CONSTRUCTION

Leghorn. First exported from Leghorn, a port in Tuscany. Made of Tuscan straw. A narrow, fine braid of thirteen strands plaited and sewed together. The joining of the braid is not visible in the plaques or shapes.

Milan. This comes from Italy and is named for the city Milan, near which most of the braid is produced. It is used for both machine and handmade hats. It is pliant and less likely to break than liséré in hand sewing. The genuine Italian Milan has a very fine weave. The imitation patent Milan is grown and plaited in China.

Milan hemp. A fine hemp woven to imitate Milan braids.

Novelties. Chenille braids; combinations of chenilles with silk floss, metals, yarns, etc. Felt cut in strips is combined with other materials.

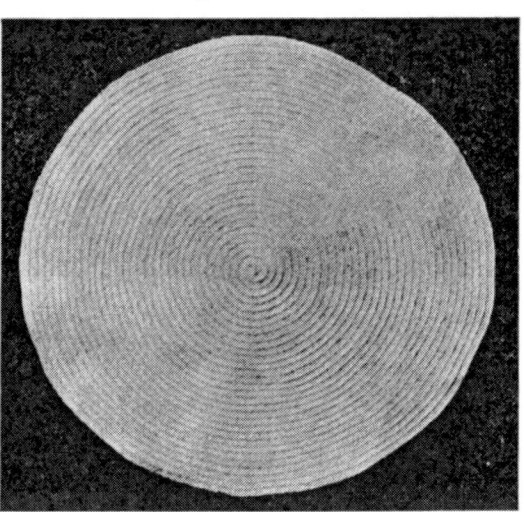

FIG. 22. *Tagal plaque*

Panama. Not a braid in the usual sense. It is a well-known kind of hat woven in a continuous shape and blocked. The city of Panama is the distributing center. Japan makes an imitation Panama. Strips from the leaves of a certain palm are used for the plaiting. A good Panama shows more knots or patched places and has little artificial stiffening. Its value is determined by fineness of weave.

Pyroxylin. An imitation of horse hair. It is a manufactured product of glucose or cellulose composition. Pyroxylin is the lightest of all braids in weight. It is not quite so stiff or so elastic

36 HATS AND HOW TO MAKE THEM

as hair braid and has a glossy appearance. It is used for transparent hats. Often the braid is folded through the middle and sewed to the hat in a series of folds, making a soft finish.

Tagal (Fig. 22, page 35). A fine quality of hemp from Italy, Japan, and the Philippines, made from abacá fiber into plateaux.

Timbo braid. Braid of rough weave which resembles Tagal slightly. It is made of hemp.

Tuscan. This braid comes from Tuscany. It is made from fine wheat straw, and the entire straw is plaited; that is, the straw is not split. The color is yellowish tan, which grows darker with age. It is a lacy-looking straw used for pressed hats, brims, and plaques. Sometimes it is made into braid (Fig. 23, upper braid) and sold by the bolt.

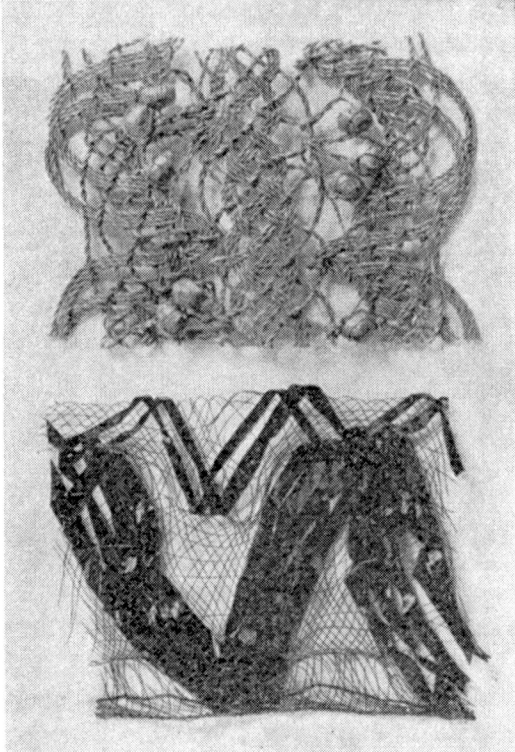

FIG. 23. *Upper: Tuscan braid;
lower: Swiss hair and visca*

Visca. Like pyroxylin, visca is a synthetic or manufactured material. It is made in a ribbonlike strip $\frac{1}{8}$ inch or more in width and is interwoven in braids and straw cloths. Commonly used. May be combined with such materials as straw, cotton thread, yarn, felt, chenille, silk, etc. Its cost depends upon the materials with which it is interwoven.

MATERIALS FOR CONSTRUCTION

Yedda. A smooth-looking straw, very pliable. It may be purchased in plaque form or as pressed hats.

Zipper. A wheat straw difficult to manipulate. To make it pliable, roll it in damp paper about two hours before using.

FABRICS

All the following materials are used from time to time for covering or trimming hats, according to the mode.

Beaver cloth. A soft woolen cloth imitating fur. It has a shaggy surface and drapes well. Comes in strips 18 inches wide and 36 inches long.

Broadcloth. A soft woolen cloth with nap laid in one direction. Width, 50 and 54 inches.

Chiffon. Used for veils, transparent hats, and trimmings. Chiffon cloth is firmer than chiffon. Width, 40 inches.

Crêpe (cotton). Used as an interlining for covering frames. All colors. Width, 27 inches.

Crêpe de Chine. Either all-silk or cotton-and-silk crêpe de Chine may be used for lining or for covering hats. Width, 36 and 40 inches.

Duvetyn (pr. düv′tēn). Soft, napped silk material with beautiful texture. Combines well with other fabrics. Width, 38 and 40 inches. Wool duvetyn is heavier and more bulky. Width, 54 inches.

Faille (Fr. pr. fä′y′; English pr. fāl). Soft, flat-ribbed silk or ribbon. Ribs or cords are wider and flatter than grosgrain.

Felt. Found most often in men's hats, for which there is a staple demand. Women's felt hats are in vogue from time to time. The best grades are made from fur (beaver), nutria, muskrat, and rabbit. The poorer ones may be made from wool and even from shoddy and cotton. The quality is measured by the softness of the felt and the beauty of the surface.

When felt hats are fashionable, they are usually pressed forms, but may be constructed from felt bought by the yard.

Georgette. Thin, dull, crêpe-like silk goods used for entire hats, facings, transparent hats, and trimmings. Plain colors or printed. Width, 40 inches.

Gingham. Used for garden or sports hats. Makes washable hats for children. Often combined with organdy. Width, 32 and 36 inches.

Grosgrain (pr. grō′grān). A heavy, corded silk or ribbon.

Hatter's plush. A silk plush with a thin pile and a high luster. Pile laid flat. Width, 21 and 40 inches.

Leather. Genuine or artificial leather may be used for sports hats or for novelty trimmings. Patent leather, suède, and many other finishes are used.

Maline. Used for transparent hats and trimmings. Similar to net, but thinner and very stiff. Much of it is treated chemically to withstand moisture. Width, 24 and 27 inches.

Messaline. Soft, lightweight satin. Width, 36 inches.

Metal cloth. Imitation of cloth of gold and silver cloth. Made from composition tinsel wound around cotton and woven. Lace is made also of metal yarns — silver, gold, and steel. Width, 24 and 36 inches.

Net. Bobbinet in silk or cotton most common. Filet and novelty nets may be used. Maline and tulle belong with the nets. Width, 36 and 72 inches.

Oilcloth. Sometimes used for sports hats or for novelty trimmings.

Organdy. Used for summer hats and for flower making. Plain or printed. Width, 36 to 70 inches.

Ottoman. A heavy, corded silk or ribbon. Ribs are larger than in grosgrain and are usually cotton covered with silk warp.

Peau de soie (pr. pō dē swä′). A heavy, leatherlike silk with a satiny surface. Used in black for mourning hats or for tailored trimmings. Width, 21 and 36 inches.

Ribbons. There are many novelty effects in ribbons every season. The following types are standard: taffeta, satin (single-

MATERIALS FOR CONSTRUCTION

and double-faced), moiré, faille, grosgrain, velvet (cotton-back, satin-back, and double-faced). There are wash ribbons for lingerie and picot-edge ribbons. Designs may be made by yarn-dyed stripes, checks, or plaids, by printing the warp or the woven ribbon, or by weaving figures with the same or contrasting colors.

The ligne is the unit of measurement for widths in ribbon. It is less than $\frac{1}{8}$ inch. Twelve lignes equal $1\frac{1}{16}$ inches (Fig. 24).

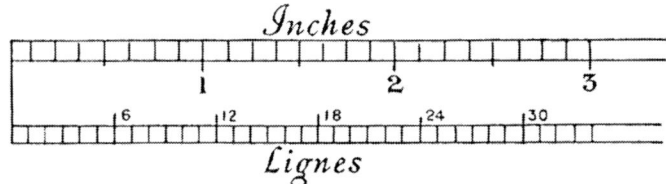

FIG. 24. *Comparison of inches and lignes*

Most of the manufacturers maintain the standard widths indicated on the accompanying scale up to No. 80 ribbon. Beyond this width there is less uniformity.

The number of the ribbon with its corresponding width in lignes is as follows:

No. 1	2 lignes	No. 12	21 lignes
No. 1½	3 lignes	No. 16	25 lignes
No. 2	4 lignes	No. 22	30 lignes
No. 3	6 lignes	No. 30	32 lignes
No. 4	8 lignes	No. 40	35 lignes
No. 5	10 lignes	No. 50	37 lignes
No. 7	13 lignes	No. 60	40 lignes
No. 9	17 lignes	No. 80	45 lignes

Bolts of ribbon are usually marked 9 meters, which is a little less than ten yards.

Satin. Used for hats, for trimmings, and for flower making. Often combined with other materials. Width, 36 inches.

Taffeta. Used for entire hats, trimmings, flowers, and linings. Width, 36 and 40 inches.

Tulle. Similar to maline and having a softer finish. Used chiefly for wedding veils. Width, 36, 72, and 108 inches.

Veiling. A general term which refers to a variety of nets, plain and fancy. Sold by the yard or in pattern lengths.

Velvet. A variety of velvets may be used for hat making and trimmings.

Velveteen is not a true velvet, but is usually considered in the same class. Velveteen is 18, 20, and 21 inches wide.

Costume velvet (cotton) may be used for sports hats. Costume velvet is 27, 36, and 40 inches wide.

Chiffon velvet is thin silk velvet with pile laid flat. Width, 40 and 50 inches.

Millinery or hat velvet is often called Lyons velvet. It may be all silk or have a cotton back. Pile is usually upright and may be thick or thin. Width, $17\frac{1}{2}$, 18, 19, and 24 inches.

Panne velvet has a heavier and closer pile than chiffon velvet. Pile is laid flat and polished to give luster. Width, 18 and 36 inches.

Paon velvet is heavier than panne, with more pile, which is also laid flat. Width, 18 inches.

Velours. Refers to a heavily napped fur hat and to a woolen fabric.

FURS

Beaver. A brown, thick, short-haired fur. Quality depends upon color and luster. Becomes matted and curly if worn in damp weather.

Coney. Rabbit fur. Some imported rabbits produce beautiful fur which is used to imitate seal and other furs.

Ermine. A short, white, lustrous fur from a small animal. Tails have dark tips. Symbol of royalty. Occasionally cat and rabbit fur is sheared and finished to imitate ermine.

Mink. Light brown, short-haired fur. Fades in the sun.

Mole. Soft, delicate, warm-gray fur from small animal. A beautiful texture to wear next to the face.

MATERIALS FOR CONSTRUCTION

Monkey. Long, black, silky, fringelike hairs. Sometimes used for edge finishes and pompons. Imitated by dyed mohair. Genuine monkey fur may be identified by the skin foundation.

Seal. Genuine seal is always sheared, dyed, and finished. Very expensive. Dyed muskrat (Hudson seal) and dyed rabbit are used to imitate seal.

Squirrel. Siberian squirrel is a beautiful, soft gray fur. Inferior grades show a yellow cast. Rabbit fur may be used to imitate squirrel.

PART IV. MAKING THE HAT

CHAPTER V

MOLDED FRAMES

MATERIALS: Preparation of materials

PLACING PATTERN ON WILLOW

HEADSIZE: Wiring—Band

SHAPING BRIM: Brim Edge Wiring—Edge Binding—Cutting Bias

MOLDING BRIMS WITHOUT PATTERNS: Rolling and Upturning Brim—Edge Finishing—Crinoline Brim

CROWNS: Materials—Crown Mold—Stretching Material on Mold—Soft Crowns of Crinoline—Band for Soft Crowns—Band with Stiff Tip—Band with Soft Tip—Sectional Crowns—Soft Crowns in One Piece—Plain Band with Full Tip

There are many satisfactory methods of making hat frames. The simplest way is to buy a commercial frame of wire, buckram, willow, or elastic net and alter it to suit the wearer. The inexperienced worker may do this, but her choice of designs will be limited. The following methods permit greater freedom in modeling:

1. *Frames to be covered:*
    a. Make wire frame (for transparent hats).
    b. Make pattern and from this make willow or buckram frame.
2. *Molds on which frames are built:*
    a. Make stiff paper mold.
    b. Use commercial buckram brim and brace with extra wires.
    c. Use wire brim. Brace with extra wires and cover with crinoline or outing flannel.
    d. For crown use commercial buckram frame and brace with wires.
    e. Buy a crown mold (wooden or metal).
3. *Free-hand molding for brim.* (No pattern required.)
4. *Molded frames*: It is possible to dampen and stretch material, like willow, buckram, crinoline, or elastic net, over a mold so that it will assume any shape desired. Molds may be made of wire, buckram, or willow.

MOLDED FRAMES

MATERIALS

The materials required for molding frames comprise: buckram or willow, Panama cloth, elastic net or rice net, wire, mull, crinoline or cambric, strong cotton thread, needles, pins, scissors, pliers, and thimble.

When marking patterns, note how the hat is to be worn on the head and mark front *F*, back *B*, right side *RS*, and left side *LS*.

Preparation of materials. If the brim is to be cut from a pattern and made without the use of a mold, cut a square of material (willow or buckram) 1 inch larger than the pattern, steam or dampen it with a cloth, and press it dry. This helps to prevent the shape from warping in the process of making.

PLACING PATTERN ON WILLOW

Place willow on a table with crinoline side down. Pin pattern to willow on woody fiber side. (This will bring crinoline side next to the hair.) If there are right and left sides of the hat, take care to place the pattern correctly.

Cut the material as directed in "Cutting Brim" (page 13), but do not turn the little slashed pieces up until the wire is sewed to headsize line.

If the brim is drooping or upturning, it will require shaping which necessitates a seam. Pin and sew the two edges. Overlap ½ inch (the allowance for making).

HEADSIZE

Measure wire as directed on page 13 for headsize plus 2 or 3 inches for overlapping. Form a circle of the wire, joining the ends with thread or tie wire. Place the two hands in the circle and pull, forming an ellipse. Try wire headsize on the head to be sure that it fits at the sides and is large enough from front to back.

Pin this wire on top of the frame from front to back. Place joinings at center back. This head wire may be smaller or larger than the original pattern line. Do not change lines of wire to conform to lines of pattern. As suggested before, the headsize must fit easily from back to front and rather closely on the sides.

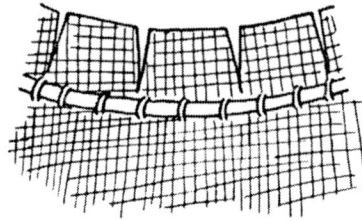

FIG. 25. *Sewing wire to headsize with stab stitch*

To have the hat large enough when finished there must be space between the forehead, and the hatband. If two fingers can be placed between the headband and the forehead, the headsize will not be too small when finished.

Wiring headsize. Hold left hand inside of headline, the thumb resting on the wire. Begin to sew at the center back, with stab stitch (Fig. 25). Sew through and back again over wire, going from right to left. Take stab stitch straight over wire, placing stitches about $\frac{1}{2}$ inch apart.

If any irregularity results from placing the headsize wire, trim within $\frac{3}{4}$ inch, slash, and bend the pieces up as directed (page 19).

Try frame on head to see if size is correct. If a mistake has been made, it will be necessary to change the frame so as to make the headsize larger or smaller.

Headsize band. Cut a piece of willow or buckram straight or bias, $\frac{3}{4}$ inch wide, the circumference of headsize plus 1 inch. Begin at back and sew this strip to outside of the little slashed pieces on top of brim. This gives additional strength to the brim (Fig. 26), and causes the slashed pieces to stand erect. Be sure this band is sewed securely to the little strips.

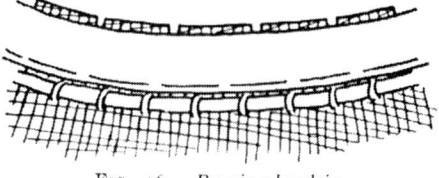

FIG. 26. *Bracing headsize*

Before placing edge wire take care that edge of brim is smooth all around. Irregular places due to bad cutting would show in the finished hat.

MOLDED FRAMES

SHAPING BRIM

If the brim is to be other than a sailor or drooping effect, shaping must be done before the edge wire is put in place. Steam or moisten willow slightly on woody side and mold it with the fingers to the desired shape. If slightly dampened, it will not break. Medium-weight willow can be shaped easily without being moistened. Heavy willow is more difficult to handle. If decided bends are used on brim, do not make them before wiring edge.

Brim edge wiring. Measure the circumference of the brim and cut a piece of wire 3 or 4 inches longer than this measurement. Straighten wire slightly by running it through the fingers. Begin at center back and sew with wire stitch, blanket stitch, buttonhole stitch, or overcasting. (See stitches, pages 91–94). There is a difference of opinion as to whether the wire should be attached to the upper or the under edge of the brim. On the whole, the former is better.

Sew wire to the upper side, i. e., place wire on top of willow, close to edge. Do not let wire extend beyond willow. Sew wire and willow securely together, being careful not to let the frame get out of shape. Make stitches from $\frac{1}{4}$ to $\frac{1}{2}$ inch apart.

A beginner is likely to stretch the willow or other material at the edge. If this occurs, the hat will assume a warped shape. To remedy this, open up edge wire for 2 or 3 inches at center back

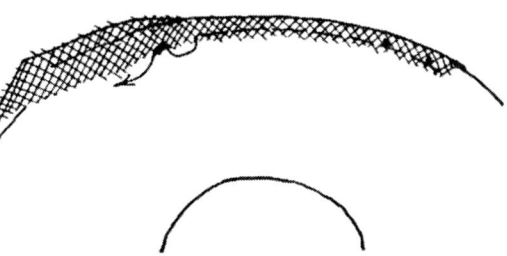
FIG. 27. *Binding edge of brim with cambric or muslin*

and slip material along, holding wire in the other hand. This will make the brim firmer so that it will lend itself to shaping.

Edge binding. The edge of the brim should be bound with a bias fold of crinoline, cambric, or mull whether it is wired or not (Fig. 27).

Cutting bias. Cut a true bias (see page 95) of crinoline $1\frac{1}{2}$ inches wide. Fold this piece through the center, with $\frac{3}{4}$ inch on each side. Place fold over edge of hat and stick a pin straight through to hold it in place. Hold right hand at point near pin and with left hand stretch material until all fullness is out of inner edge. Be careful not to misshape hat when stretching crinoline. No fullness should be left at inner edge. This can be removed only by stretching. With stab stitch sew through and back again very near edges of crinoline. Make stitches from $\frac{1}{4}$ to $\frac{1}{2}$ inch long, with occasional backstitch.

MOLDING BRIMS WITHOUT PATTERNS

The free-hand method is a popular way of making frames, and many interesting shapes may be formed from Panama cloth, elastic net, or crinoline. The first two materials lend themselves to soft, close-fitting, and medium-sized hats. Crinoline is appropriate for small sailor, drooping, or slightly rolling effects. Sports hats with crinoline foundations may be made successfully from crinoline without wiring.

Rolling and upturning brim. Make headsize band first by cutting a straight piece of willow, buckram, or any other stiff material $\frac{3}{4}$ inch wide and equal in length to size of head, plus 2 inches for overlapping. This forms a support for the brim. The wire must be sewed to *outside* of band. Overlap wire from 2 to 3 inches. Pull this band to an ellipse so as to fit the head.

Cut a bias piece of Panama cloth or elastic net the width of brim desired, plus 2 inches for making. The length cannot be determined unless a hat is being copied. On one side of this bias strip make slashes $\frac{3}{4}$ inch deep and 1 inch apart. This will permit more fullness to be forced into the headsize.

Begin at back and pin slashed edge of elastic net or Panama cloth to the inside of headsize. Force bias piece into headsize and pin it in place. (The more fullness there is forced into the

MOLDED FRAMES 47

headsize, the straighter the brim.) Cut ends so there will be an overlap from 1 to 2 inches. Pin and sew the ends together. If necessary, remove fullness in headsize by steaming and pressing. If a rolling brim is desired, turn material up after adjusting it to headsize, and trim to desired width.

Edge finishing. If the edge is to be wired, the brim can be made to roll more if material is held full when sewing wire on. The material may be turned down on the edge $\frac{1}{2}$ inch and the wire

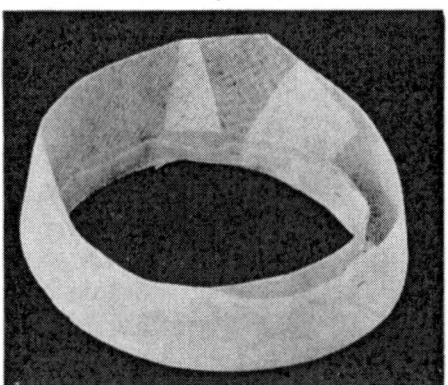 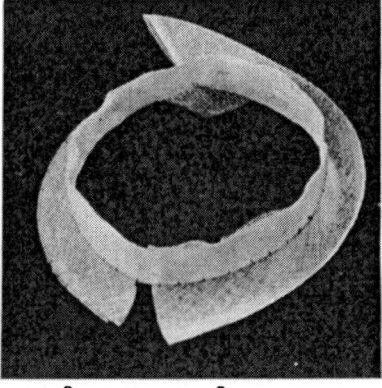

FIG. 28. *Free-hand molding of frame: (1) elastic net—bias strip with gusset; (2) crinoline wired for straight brim; (3) soft roll, not wired*

sewed into the fold. A row of machine stitching may be placed on the outer edge of the bias strip, before it is sewed to headsize, to prevent stretching.

If more of a flare is desired on the brim, steam, stretch, and press it on the edge. Wire and bind it with a bias fold of crinoline or cambric. Wire may be omitted and only binding used for a soft edge.

To make a small shape, such as a turban, do not fold material in at headsize, but hold it slack while working. To obtain irregular shapes force the net into place at various points on the headsize. For example, if the net is forced into place on each side, leaving the back and front plain, the sides will flare and the back and front turn almost erect. If more of a flare or irregularity is desired, slash from edge to headsize and insert a little gusset. Pin in gusset, observe effect, and sew it in place (Fig. 28, No. 1, page 47).

Crinoline brim. Cut a bias fold of crinoline twice the width of brim desired, plus 1 inch for making. Determine length by headsize plus 2 inches for overlapping. Fold width in the middle. Use crown or a band as directed (page 46).

Pin and sew crinoline to underside of band or crown as for elastic net. Stretch edge of crinoline to make a straight-brim sailor. Wire and bind (Fig. 28, No. 2). A soft roll or irregular-shaped brim may be made without the wire. This method furnishes opportunity for originality.

CROWNS

Owing to the constant change in style there are various ways of making crowns. The mode dictates whether a crown must be high or low, slanting or straight-sided, soft or stiff. Fashion dictates whether the crown shall be made in two pieces, like the paper crown; in several sections; in tam effect; or blocked in one piece. Study the various types of crowns each season to keep up to date. Many crowns are made on a foundation that conforms to the shape of the head. The finished crown may have any outline desired, such as a tam or draped effect.

Materials. Elastic net, crinoline, and Panama cloth are all used from time to time for crowns. They are adaptable for freehand blocking or steaming and drawing over a frame. (See directions for steaming and blocking crowns, page 50.)

If a stiff effect is desired, use buckram or rice net or combine both, using rice net for tip and buckram for side crown.

Willow is not a good material for an entire crown, as it breaks too easily. It may be used, however, for narrow side bands, which are often placed on underside at the base of the crown for additional support.

MOLDED FRAMES

Crown mold. Wooden molds may be purchased or made to order. A carpenter, cabinet maker, or manual training teacher can make a block from cedar, copying the modern crown. Blocks of copper net or plain metal may be purchased. If neither of the above molds is available, buy a buckram crown and wire it as follows:

1. With stab stitch sew a piece of medium-sized wire on the underside of frame from front to back, dividing frame in half. Follow carefully the lines of the crown. Extend support wires 1 inch from each side of crown base. With pliers bend the 1 inch of wire parallel to base of crown and overcast securely.
2. Divide crown into quarters and eighths by adding four wires, bending and sewing the ends of the wire as directed above.

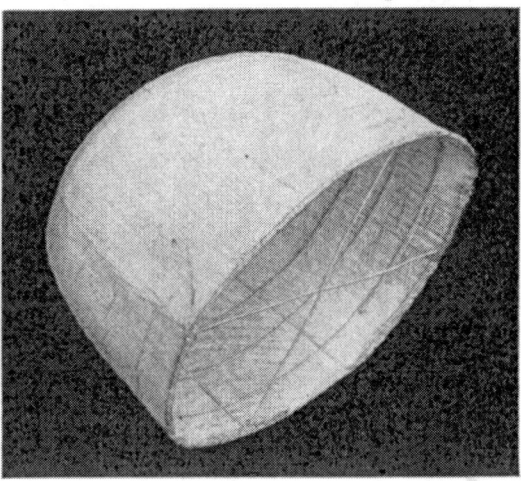

FIG. 29. *Commercial frame wired for mold*

3. On underside begin at center back, about $\frac{1}{2}$ or $\frac{3}{4}$ inch from base, and sew a brace wire around crown parallel to base. Overlap wire 2 inches at center back.
4. To strengthen the crown further, sew other wires in the same manner. Space wires equally from base to tip, but not more than $\frac{3}{4}$ inch apart. At center of tip make an ellipse about 2 or 3 inches in diameter.
5. Put on two additional brace wires at the base: (1) diameter of base of crown from front to back; (2) the diameter from side to side. Cut the wires about 2 inches longer than

the base. Bend 1 inch on each end of wire and sew parallel to lower edge of crown. These extra braces will hold the crown securely.

A crown wired in this manner makes an excellent block for the home milliner who does not wish to invest in a wooden or

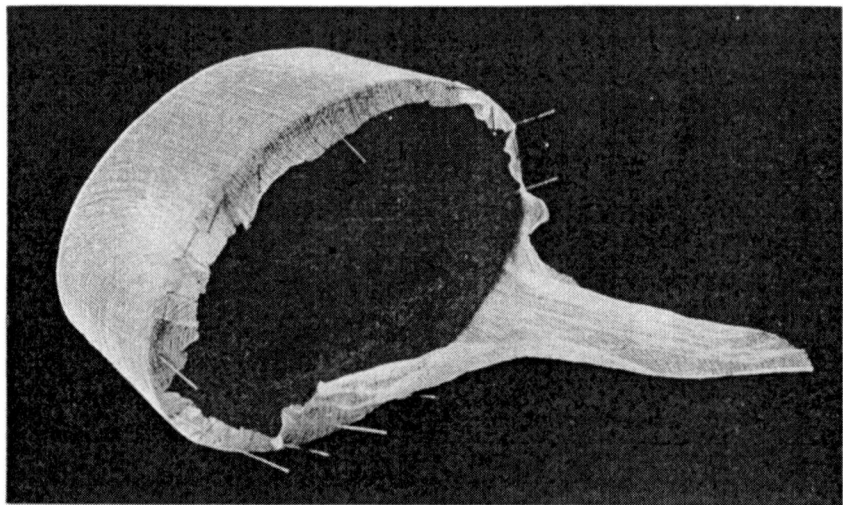

FIG. 30. *Crinoline molded over wooden block*

metal mold (Fig. 29, page 49). A buckram brim may be wired and used as a mold in the same way.

Stretching material on mold. Cut a square of material 1 inch larger than the longest diameter of the crown, measuring over top of crown. Pin straight of material to front, back, and sides over top. Hold crown over a steam kettle or exhaust pipe, or moisten it slightly, and stretch it on the bias. Pull material from straight to bias (Fig. 30). With little effort stretching will remove all fullness.

Remove crown from block. For wooden or buckram blocks it is advisable to have a piece of whalebone to loosen material gradually from the mold. If whalebone is not convenient, use a long pin or needle.

MOLDED FRAMES

Trim lower edge of crown. Then cut a band about 2 inches wide of stiff material such as buckram, willow, or elastic net the same circumference as the crown. Place on underside and pin the two materials together. Wire and bind bottom of crown as for edge of brim. In case side band slopes, this band of stiff material must slope accordingly.

Soft crowns of crinoline. Use the pattern cut for the paper hat, either with straight or curved side band and tip. Cut material as directed for the paper work, but make allowances for seams on side band as well as tip. It is not necessary to slash edge of tip as suggested for paper work. (See page 22.)

Begin at center back of tip and sew band around edge, holding band next to worker. The band and tip may be basted and stitched on the machine or sewed with small running stitches. Overlap and sew the two ends. Turn the crown inside out, and fit it to the brim to see whether height and size are satisfactory. Turn the lower edge under and attach a wire.

Many crowns have a piece of willow, elastic net, buckram, or some other form of stiff material cut about 2 inches wide with the circumference of the side band. It may be either straight or curved, depending upon the style of crown side band. Place this piece on underside of band and sew a wire to lower edge, joining the two. Bind as for edges of brim.

Band for soft crowns. Cut a strip of stiff material on the bias, straight, or curved, the size and width desired. Join ends, wire the band, and bind lower edge. Shape this band in the hands until it fits over the headsize. Make outside crown any desired shape, place it on brim, and attach.

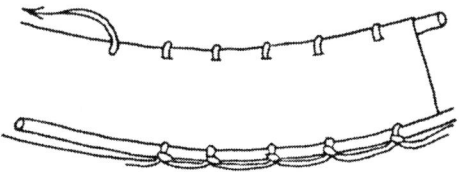
FIG. 31. *Band with stiff tip. Crown edge and base of side band wired*

Band with stiff tip. Wire both sides of side band, i. e., crown edge and base (Fig. 31). Wire tip on underside near edge and attach it to band. Then join the band. The joining should come at center back. Bind crown edge (see Glossary) and base with a bias piece of mull or crinoline as for edge of brim.

Band with soft tip. The above band may be used with a tip of soft material. The tip may be cut the diameter of the band plus the making, or larger, forming fullness. Attach tip to top of band. A variety of tips may be obtained by the use of Panama cloth or elastic net. Cut an ellipse about 2 inches larger than the *diameter* of the *band* and divide band into halves, quarters, and eighths. Push tip through band from underside. Pin division marks on tip in line with those on band. This causes fullness of ellipse above band to give a rounded effect to top of crown.

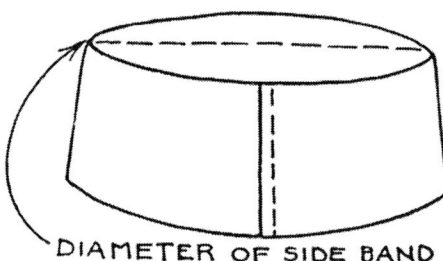

FIG. 32. *Band with soft tip. Side band joined*

Sectional crowns. See pattern instructions, page 23.

Soft crowns in one piece. See pattern instructions, page 24.

Plain band with full tip. See pattern instructions, page 23.

CHAPTER VI

WIRE FRAMES

    MATERIALS: Preparation for Work—Use of Tie Wire
    MEASUREMENTS: Head—Brim—Wire
    CONSTRUCTION
    HEADSIZE WIRE: Shaping
    SUPPORT OR SPOKE WIRES: Attaching Headsize to Spoke Wires
    SAILOR FRAME: Measuring Wires—Wiring Edge—Fastening Edge Wire to Spokes—Brace Wires
    MUSHROOM OR DROOPING BRIM: Edge Wire—Brace Wires
    UPTURNING OR ROLLING BRIM: Shaping Frame—Wiring Edge
    UPTURNING BRIM WITH SLASH ON SIDE: Measurements—Brace Wire
    MOLD FOR IRREGULAR SHAPE: Preparing Wire Frame for Mold
    COVERING FRAME: Finishing Edge—Making Seam—Cutting Headsize
    MOLDING WILLOW OVER WIRE: Removing from Frame—Finishing Edge
    MOLDING OVER PAPER
    WIRE CROWN MOLDS AND FRAMES: Measurements Used in Illustration—Making Wire Crown Mold—Covering Mold with Crinoline—Making Wire Crown Frame

The question is often asked, "What is the most important thing to learn about millinery?" There is but one answer: "The making of wire frames." This work is the basis for practically all frame making. It is indispensable for the worker who copies models or creates her own designs. The copyist may reproduce any exclusive model by exact wire-frame making, The wire frame serves as a block for molding willow, buckram, rice-net frames, etc. Transparent hats make the wire frame useful at all seasons of the year. For this style, the frame may be covered with organdy, georgette, lace, maline, or hair braid. The frame is made in two pieces, brim and crown. Each piece is covered separately as for fabric hats, then joined.

MATERIALS

Good workmanship in frame making requires suitable materials. The following will be found essential: (1) roll of medium-sized silk-covered frame wire; (2) spool of tie wire; (3) pair of good pliers with pointed ends; (4) tape measure; (5) pencil; (6) scissors.

Preparation for work. Hold coil of wire over one hand and with pliers remove the two little pieces binding the coil. Be careful not to let the coil spring out at the center after removing these pieces. Place the coil between the hands or over the arm and shake it until it is uniformly loosened. Practice cutting wire by placing it well into the jaws of the pliers and clipping firmly without sawing or pulling. Continue to practice until you can cut wires at one stroke by pressing directly down. Straighten wires to remove some of the spring by passing the wire between the outstretched thumb and fingers, thus bending it slightly in the opposite direction from curve of wire. Or, pass wire lightly through the hand to straighten it. Be careful not to put little kinks in the wire, because these make it more difficult to handle.

Use of tie wire. Remove a short length at a time and keep end of tie wire fastened, or it will spring from spool. To gauge lengths of wire suitable for joinings, wind several pieces around two fingers, slightly apart, and make an elongated loop. Remove wire from fingers and cut it on both sides of the ellipse, making pieces 1 inch or more long.

MEASUREMENTS

Head measurement. Take close measurement of head where the hat will rest, plus 1 inch for making and 2 inches for overlapping. The average commercial frame measures 24 inches at the base.

Brim measurement. Take brim measurements by placing tape measure on underside of frame at headsize, then pass the tape to edge of frame. The measurements must be taken at four

WIRE FRAMES

or eight places, front, back, right, and left sides, then between side fronts and side backs. The style of frame will determine the number of measurements to be taken.

For a regular shape cut wires the width of brim plus 3 inches.

For an irregular shape cut all wires the length of the longest plus 3 inches; or measure and cut each wire, placing the wires to the headsize in the order of cutting—back, front, sides, etc. When copying a hat exactly, measure its circumference; or determine the size after edge wire has been placed on frame. Straighten edge wire slightly before attaching it.

Wire measurement. Always straighten wire before measuring it; or measure it by placing tape on *outside* curve. Be exact in all measurements.

CONSTRUCTION

The brim and crown are made separately as in previous work. Measurements may be taken from a hat; or a paper pattern may be made and adjusted to the head.

Take the pattern as a basis for measurements for the wire frame, or make an original shape by placing a skeleton frame on the head and measuring support or spoke wires the required distance from head for size of frame. Measure front wire first, then side, then back, etc. The diagonals may be gauged according to length of front, back, and side wires.

HEADSIZE WIRE

Measure carefully on outer curve of wire and cut a piece the size of head plus the making; for example, 24 inches plus 2 inches for overlap. With pliers bend wire slightly at the 24-inch size, or mark the point with pencil or chalk. Take some of the spring from the wire by drawing it between the fingers. Join this piece of wire in a circle by overlapping the ends at the 2-inch marking. Use short lengths of tie wire as suggested (page 54) and twist them once or twice around the joining of wire about

¼ inch from each end. Fasten by taking ends of tie wire in each hand and twisting it tightly one, two, or three times. Give an

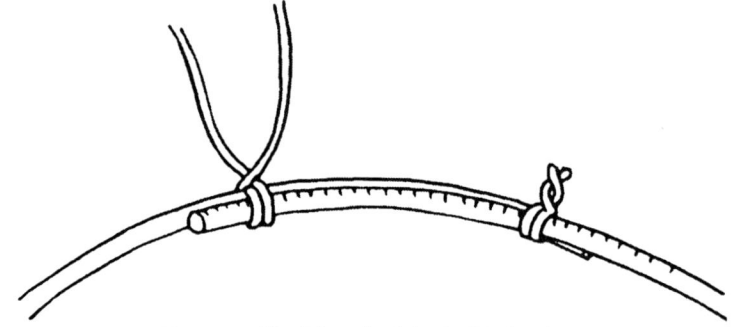

FIG. 33. *Headsize wire joined with tie wire*

additional twist with pliers, but do not twist too often or the wire will break. Cut the little upstanding ends of wire, leaving ⅛ inch or less (Fig. 33). Press these flat with pliers. Fasten both ends of overlap in the same manner. In the absence of tie wire, heavy thread will answer the purpose. Wrap it around the wire two or three times and tie. Use a second headsize wire as above, but make it ½ inch smaller, i. e., 23½ inches.

Shaping headsize. Overlap the two wires and join them. Place the hands on the inside of the two wires, one at center front, the other at center back, and pull the circle to form an ellipse. Try the 24-inch piece on the head to test for size. Also be sure that the wire touches the head at the sides. (Read previous instructions for fitting the head, page 44.) If headsize wire is too large or too small, alter it.

SUPPORT OR SPOKE WIRES

Measure and cut eight spoke wires the width of the brim plus making. If the brim measures 3½ inches all around, cut wires 6½ inches. Two inches of the three allowed for making will be used at the headsize for connecting the two pieces. The extra inch is to twist around the edge wire holding the two together.

WIRE FRAMES

Straighten the wire as suggested above by drawing it between the fingers. Bend wires 2 inches from one end of each spoke wire.

Attaching headsize to spoke wires (Fig. 34). Hold the 24-inch headsize wire at the center joining and place the spoke wire on the underside of headsize piece at the bend of the 2-inch length. The spoke must run at right angles to the headsize. Hold the two firmly together between the finger and thumb of the left hand. With the right hand bend the 2-inch piece upright. Press end straight forward and downward so that one piece of wire lies parallel with the other. Twist just enough to the right side to allow wire to pass back and up. When the twist is finished, the wires will lie parallel and close to each other. Unless the headsize wire is kept close in the bend of spoke while you are twisting it, it may loosen and be difficult to tighten with pliers.

Divide headsize into halves, quarters, and eighths, marking the points. Attach front wire at halfway mark, the two sides at quarter marks, and remaining wires halfway between these. Be careful that each spoke wire is at right angles to headsize wire. The spoke wires will bend slightly downward, giving a lamp-shade effect.

Measure 1 inch from the base or headsize wire on the 2-inch wire standing up around the frame. Bend this wire toward the center of head piece at right angles and opposite the first bend. Measure the $23\frac{1}{2}$-inch headsize wire and divide it in quarters as above. Place this wire above base wire and close into bend of back piece.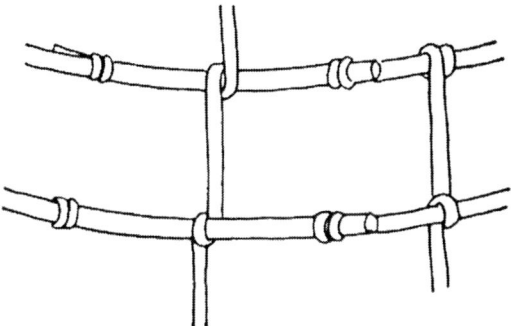

FIG. 34. *Attaching spoke wires to headsize wires*

Be careful to place joinings at back, one above the other. Hold headsize close to bend of upright wire and twist wire as before. Press downward and forward, then straight up, following the above instructions. Place the front wire, then the two sides, causing the two headsize wires to separate from $\frac{3}{4}$ to 1 inch. To lower head piece tighten spoke wires by pressing them with point of pliers. Cut end from top piece as close as possible. Hold pliers parallel with head piece and press tightly. At this point all wires must be fastened so that the frame is solid.

SAILOR FRAME

Hold right hand inside head piece from top side and proceed to bring each wire to desired shape with left hand. Bend wires from downward lamp-shade shape to wheel effect with eight straight spokes. Examine wires from underside to see that front and back wires are opposite, or as though in a continuous straight line. The sides and diagonals must be opposite each other also. For a sailor the spokes should tend to turn up rather than down.

Measuring wires. Place hand inside head piece and with middle finger hold tape measure just even with headline on front wire. Continue tape measure to the desired size (for example, 3 inches). Mark with pencil, or bend wire upright. Measure and mark the remaining seven wires in the same manner. A pencil mark is preferable to a bend in the wire.

Wiring edge. Note how the hat is to be placed on the head. Begin to work from the left side at the back. Straighten an approximate length of wire for edge, then place roll of wire over top headsize wire. The end of wire must extend 4 or 5 inches on right-hand side of center-back spoke wire. With tie wire, fasten edge wire to left side-back spoke wire at the marking made for size of frame. Attach to side spoke wire, fastening with tie wire. Be careful not to force edge wire so as to spread the spokes too much. Take care that each wire radiates from headsize to edge. Continue to work around the brim. At back, overlap the two wires, drawing them together. Keep spokes as near desired shape as possible. Tie the two overlapping pieces temporarily. Cut wire from roll about 4 or 5 inches at left side of center back, causing an overlap of 8 or 10 inches. The overlap may extend to both sides of back spoke. Try the frame on the head. If the brim has a tendency to warp, the edge wire is too full. If it droops, the wire is too tight (i. e., for a sailor shape). Open edge wire at back and adjust accordingly.

Fastening edge wire to spokes. Bend the ends of spokes around edge wire as for top headsize wire. Bend each end straight out from the edge. Remove tie wire with pliers. Cut spoke ends close to underside of edge wire and press tightly. Hold pliers on a straight line with radiating spokes in tightening. Fasten each end of overlap with tie wire.

Brace wires. For a $3\frac{1}{2}$-inch brim one or two brace wires are needed on top of the frame, running in the same direction as edge wire. Begin to work at the center back as for the edge wire. Let wire extend several inches to right side of back. Tie brace and spoke wires together at left side-back about $1\frac{1}{2}$ inches from edge wire. Continue to attach brace wire around brim an equal distance from edge. Overlap it across the back and fasten it with tie wire. Twist, cut, and press the little upstanding ends of wire as directed for joining head pieces (page 56).

MUSHROOM OR DROOPING BRIM

The mushroom or drooping brim is made in the same manner as the sailor frame. Follow instructions, but in shaping the spoke wires bend them slightly downward to the lamp-shade form instead of having spokes at right angles to headsize wire. The type of face will determine the degree of droop. Each spoke may measure the same number of inches (for example, 3 inches), or back spokes may be shorter and graduate in length to front wire; or both back and front spokes may be shorter than the sides.

Edge wire. Fasten the edge wire to spokes with tie wire as suggested for the sailor. Try the shape on the head to get the desired droop. Twist, cut, and tighten spokes around edge wire.

Brace wires. Fasten brace wires on top of spoke wires, being careful to have all joinings of wire overlap center-back spoke wire. The number of braces depends on the use and size of the frame. Transparent hats are sometimes made without additional brace wires. The edge and spoke wires give sufficient foundation for the brim.

UPTURNING OR ROLLING BRIM

Make preliminary foundation as for sailor frame.

Shaping frame. Instead of bending spoke wires at right angles as for the sailor, or bending the wire down as for the mushroom droop, reverse the bending of the spokes. Bend wires with a gradual curve from headsize to edge. Place left hand inside the head wires, and put second finger of right hand near headsize, the thumb under the wire. Spread thumb and finger to give each spoke an upturning bend. Take care that each spoke wire has the same curve from headsize to edge. Do not turn the spokes abruptly up, but curve them at right angles, then gradually to the edge. For the turban, however, the spokes may curve directly from headsize.

Wiring edge. Measure brim, straighten wire, cut the length desired, and attach edge wire temporarily, as for the sailor frame. Try frame on the head to adjust spokes to edge before twisting and tightening them to finish edge of brim. Overlap edge wire across center-back wire, but before finishing see whether desired curve has been turned. If so, draw edge wire together and fasten it lightly with tie wire. Replace spokes in position to keep lines radiating. If less curve is desired, spread edge wire and replace spokes at edge. A good illustration of the upturning or rolling brim for a wire frame is shown on page 61.

WIRE FRAMES

UPTURNING BRIM WITH SLASH ON SIDE

The above instructions may be used for the upturning brim with a slash on the side with one exception. The opening (Fig. 35) is between the right side and the right side-back.

MEASUREMENTS
(See page 43 for abbreviations)

Headsize wire	24 inches
Headsize wire	23½ inches
(Add 3 inches to each spoke wire for making)	
C. B.	3¼ inches
F.	4¼ inches
L. and R. S. F.	4 inches
L. and R. S.	3¾ inches
Total circumference of edge wire	44¾ inches
Divided as follows:	
R. S. to C. F.	12 inches
to L. S.	23 inches
to C. B.	34 inches
to R. S. B.	39 inches
to bend of edge wire	41½ inches
to headsize	44¾ inches

The total circumference of the edge wire on this slashed brim is 44¾ inches plus allowance for making. Straighten edge wire slightly and begin at spoke at right side, working toward the left. Let edge wire extend 1 inch to left of spoke and fasten it temporarily with tie wire. Beginning at right-side spoke, carry tape measure along with edge wire. The distance should be 12

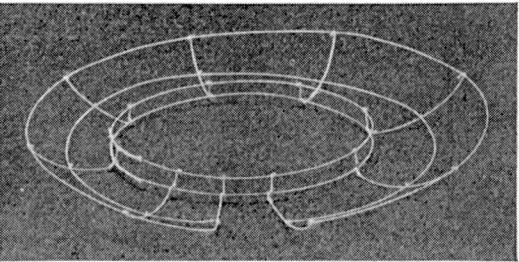

FIG. 35. *Upturning brim with slash on side*

inches from right side to center front. Do not bend spoke wire, but attach edge wire to each temporarily with tie wire. Continue tape measure with edge wire to 23 inches at left-side spoke; to 34 inches at center back; to 39 inches at right side-back; to 41 inches; then bend edge wire at right angles. Fasten edge wire to headsize at $44\frac{3}{4}$ inches; also to upper headsize wire as for other spokes. This makes the edge wire form an additional spoke which is halfway between right side and right side-back. The spoke is often added for an irregular-shaped brim.

Tie the remaining spokes (side fronts and side backs) to edge wire with tie wire.

Now bend spoke wires over edge wire as directed in "Support or Spoke Wires," page 57. Remove tie wires. Lastly, fasten edge and spoke wires at right side by twisting edge wire around spoke wire and spoke wire around edge wire as shown in Fig. 35, on page 61.

Brace wire. Place the brace wire halfway between the headsize and the edge on the top of the frame. Join them with tie wire as in shaping sailor frame, directions for which are given on page 59.

MOLD FOR IRREGULAR SHAPE

This type of irregular brim includes most of the principles of wire-frame making. It is a combination of brim and turban (Fig. 47, page 85). Notice the $\frac{5}{8}$-inch bend near headsize at front, side-front, and side wires. This causes the spokes to droop slightly and extend from the headsize line. It is known as a *facing* or *hair line*. From sides to back, there is no facing line because the spoke wires turn gradually as for an upturned brim.

The purpose of the facing line is to give the effect of increased size to the frame. Take care not to extend or bend the wires down too far or there will be too much space between head and brim. This line may be placed the same depth all around as for a turban; or it may be uneven, causing the hat to show more of the hair at one point than another.

For making a frame like the illustration use the measurements given on the following page.

WIRE FRAMES

Note that for the irregular brim two figures are given plus the 3 inches for making. The first figure is the distance from headsize on the spoke to the first bend, which makes the facing line. The second figure indicates the length of spoke to edge of finished brim measurements. (See page 43 for abbreviations.)

    Headsize wire..............................24 inches
    Headsize wire............................23½ inches
    B....................................... 1⅞ inches
    F..⅝ inch, 3⅞ inches
    R. S..................................... 2¼ inches
    L. S......................................⅝ inch, 4 inches
    R. S. F..................................⅝ inch, 3 inches
    R. S. B.................................. 1¾ inches
    L. S. F..................................⅝ inch, 4¼ inches
    L. S. B.................................. 3 inches

    Edge wire, C. B. to L. S., 9½ in.; to L. S., 13¾ in.; bend edge wire, C. F. 18¼ in.; R. S. 27 in.; to C. B. 34½ in. circumference finished. Facing line 27¾ in. circumference finished.

For details of making see page 57. After bending spoke wires to desired shape, fasten facing wire (27¾ inches circumference) to spokes with tie wire. Attach edge wire. See page 59 for directions.

Note additional brace wires in the illustration on page 85 (Fig. 47) and the uneven spacing required because of the irregularity of the brim. Continue two of the brace wires, one nearest the edge wire and the second nearest the headsize, around the brim. It is not necessary to place the remaining brace wires all around because of irregularity of the brim. Also note that the ends of the brace wires are attached to spokes by twisting. As a mold for sewing braid hats, or for molding frames of willow or rice net, it is necessary to have brace wires not more than ¾ inch apart. If the frame is irregular in shape as illustrated, it is not possible to keep brace wires at an equal distance around the frame.

HATS AND HOW TO MAKE THEM

Preparing wire frame for mold. In molding willow, buckram, elastic net, or other material over a wire frame, it is advisable to cover the frame first with crinoline, muslin, or outing flannel, preferably the first. This lessens imprints of wire on material.

COVERING FRAME

Begin on underside of frame at center front. Pin bias corner of crinoline to center front at edge of brim, then to headsize. Push fullness toward back from each side of front, pinning alternately at edge and at headsize. Steam crinoline slightly to avoid pulling the frame out of shape. It may be necessary to stretch the crinoline in the hands at certain parts of the frame to make the covering fit closely into all the corners. The covering must be perfectly smooth all around the frame. Take great care not to bend the edge wire out of position.

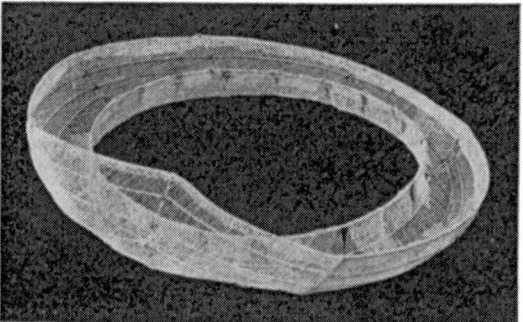

FIG. 36. *Wire frame prepared for molding*

Finishing edge. Trim crinoline $\frac{1}{4}$ or $\frac{1}{2}$ inch from edge of frame, slash it at intervals, turn to opposite side, and sew it close to wire.

Making seam. Cut material from edge to headsize, allowing $\frac{1}{2}$-inch overlap, and sew with stab stitch (page 93).

Cutting headsize. Cut crinoline about $1\frac{1}{2}$ inches from headsize, snip at $\frac{3}{4}$-inch intervals, turn the little slashed pieces over top headsize wire, and sew them in place (Fig. 36).

MOLDING WILLOW OVER WIRE

See the illustration on page 65 (Fig. 37). This method of molding will be found satisfactory for the experienced worker. It is difficult for the beginner to make a perfect wire frame on

WIRE FRAMES

which to mold. Steam willow on wood-fiber side, or place it flat on the table, and with cloth dampened in hot water moisten willow, being careful not to get it too wet. Begin with a bias corner, place

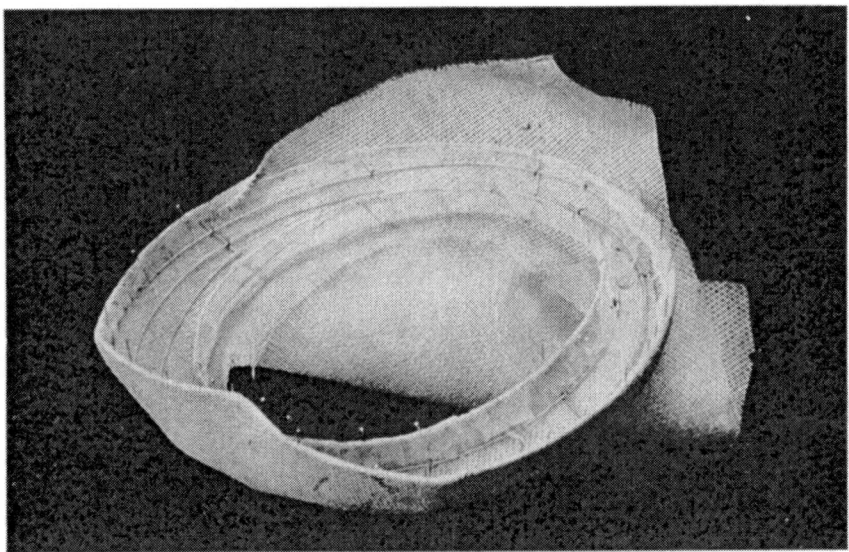

FIG. 37. *Molding willow over wire frame*

woody side next frame, and pin it to center front at edge of brim, then to headsize, and proceed as for crinoline covering.

See Fig. 37 for turning over edge at headsize and the placing of pins.

Removing from frame. When willow is

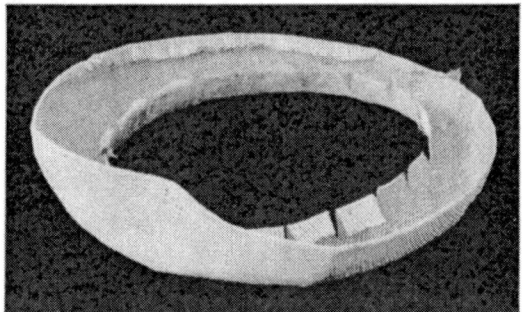

FIG. 38. *Willow removed from mold*

thoroughly dry, mark carefully the place for the seam, allowing $\frac{1}{2}$-inch overlap. Wire the frame and finish headsize. (See page 44.)

Finishing edge. Trim edge, following crease made by folding and pinning to brim. Wire and bind the edge as described on page 45. In case a soft-edge effect is desired, omit wire and bind cut edge with a bias fold of crinoline or cambric.

MOLDING OVER PAPER

To mold willow or net (elastic net or cape net) over paper, follow directions given on preceding page for molding over wire (Fig. 37, page 65).

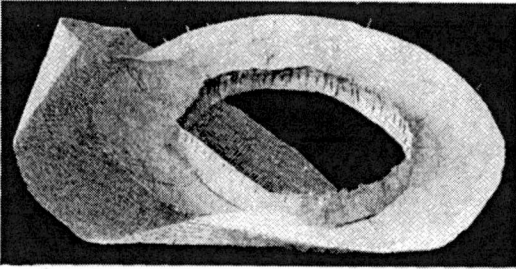

FIG. 39. *Stretching cape net over paper mold*

WIRE CROWN MOLDS AND FRAMES

The wire crown has its place in the making of hats, although its popularity varies with the demands of fashion. It is useful also as a mold for sewing braids and for molding shapes from materials. However, the mold is very difficult to make, and unless one has skill in bending the wires, it is advisable to use one of the other molds suggested (pages 49 and 50).

MEASUREMENTS USED IN ILLUSTRATIONS ON PAGE 67 (FIGS. 40 AND 41)

Base wire or crown headsize wire	25 inches
Crown edge or division wire between tip and side crown	23 inches
Side crown	3¾ inches
Tip from front to back	9 inches
Tip from side to side	7 inches
Tip diagonals (wires between sides and back and front)	8 inches

Two inches must be allowed on all brace wires (those running around the crown) for lapping, and all laps must be made at the center back. One inch must be allowed on each end of the support wires for turnings around the base wire. The wires at right angles to the brace wires are called *support wires*.

WIRE FRAMES

Straighten wire as it is taken from roll before measuring and cutting the desired length (page 55).

Making wire crown mold. Measure and cut one support wire, to be used from front to back, 18½ inches long. Measure from one end 3¾ inches plus 1 inch for making and bend the wire at the 4¾-inch mark. Measure from this bend 9 inches and bend the wire again. This gives the diameter of tip from front to back (Fig. 40). Straighten, measure, and cut the side wire 16½ inches long. Use the same side-crown measurement, 4¾ inches, but make the tip diameter from side to side 7 inches. Cut two wires for diagonals 17½ inches long, using the side-band measurement and an 8-inch diagonal.

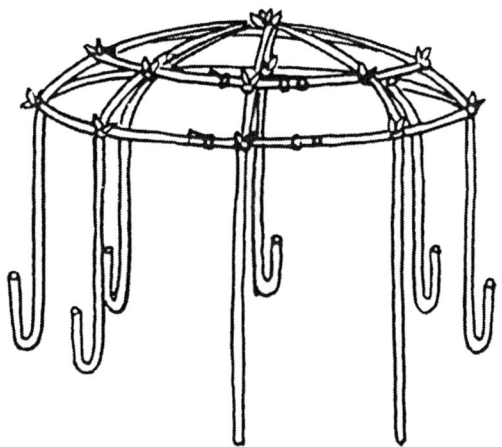

FIG. 40. *Construction of wire crown*

Curve tip wires slightly, and place them together so that all tip diameters curve in like manner with the side crown wires at right angles to the tip.

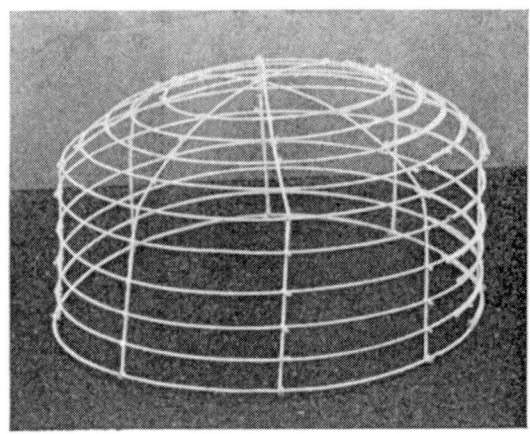

FIG. 41. *Wire mold for crown*

For the base wire, measure and cut a wire 25 inches long plus 2 inches for lapping. Fasten this with tie wire as shown on page 56. Form an ellipse and mark eight equal divisions on it, indicating center front, back, two sides, and four diagonal points.

The brace wires may be placed inside the support wires, but the measurements given require that they be placed outside. Some workers find it easier to attach the base wire first, but preference is given to the method of attaching the crown edge wire first. Place all tip wires before the base wire is attached.

Prepare the crown edge wire, measuring a length 23 inches plus 2 inches for lapping, and fasten the lap with tie wire as shown on page 56. Form an ellipse, mark eight equal divisions as on base wire, and fasten crown edge wire to bends on support wires with tie wire. Do not fasten tie wires permanently until all eight points have been attached or until a second or third wire has been placed. Fasten crossing of support wires to center of tip with tie wire.

Place tip wires next, working from crown edge wire to center crossing of support wires. Place base wires about $\frac{1}{2}$ inch apart. Be sure to fasten each overlap temporarily and shape brace wires to conform with the oval edge wire before attaching them. After all tip wires are securely fastened, measure down from the crown edge wire $3\frac{3}{4}$ inches on each support wire and bend all outward at right angles. Be sure that all support wires are straight before fastening the base wire.

Place base wire in the bends so that each support wire meets the eight divisions marked on the base wire. Turn the 1-inch extension over the base wire once only, bringing the end of the support wire in conjunction with its original position, and not at right angles.

After all support wires are turned and fastened (see page 57) the crown is ready for the side brace wires. These may be placed about $\frac{1}{2}$ inch apart. After tie wires are properly cut and bent, no sharp points should be left to catch in the frame covering. This completes the crown mold. Before molding frame material, it is advisable to cover the wire mold with crinoline, muslin, or canton flannel to lessen the impressions of the wires.

Covering mold with crinoline. (1) Cover tip first, pinning from front to back, and side to side, then at diagonals. Sew crinoline to crown edge wire, leaving only $\frac{1}{4}$-inch extension. If the tip is steamed slightly, all wrinkles can be removed. (2) Fit the crinoline smoothly around the side crown from edge wire to base, allowing $\frac{1}{2}$ inch to turn over base toward inside of crown.

Making wire crown frame. If a wire foundation is desired for transparent materials, do not use more than one brace wire between base and crown edge wire and use only one between crown edge wire and center of tip.

CHAPTER VII

ESTIMATING MATERIALS FOR HAT COVERINGS

MEASURING FOR BRIMS: Plain Brim—Other Types of Brim Coverings—Full or Shirred Brim

MEASURING FOR CROWNS: Crown with Plain Tip and Side Band

COVERING FRAME: Preparing Frame for Covering—Placing Velvet on Frame—Sewing Velvet to Brim—Facing Brim—Completing Headsize—Preparing Edge—Finishing Edge with Wire

COVERING IRREGULAR SHAPES: Joining Seam—Gluing to Frame—Replacing Covering on Brim—Underfacing Irregular Shapes—Making Hats of One Material

A knowledge of the widths of materials is necessary before one may estimate the approximate quantity for a hat. The type of hat, whether tailored or draped, must be decided also. The following are standard widths for materials commonly used:

Velvet.................................18, 22, 40 inches
Duvetyn...............................36, 42 inches
Hatter's plush.........................19, 22, 24 inches
Satin and taffeta......................36, 40 inches

MEASURING FOR BRIMS

Plain brim. If a hat covering is to be plain, measure on the underside at the point of greatest diameter, as directed in measurements for paper patterns. In this case allow 1 to 2 inches for making. If the brim is to be covered with the same material on both sides, it will take twice the width of the brim at the widest point. For example, the brim of a hat 16 inches in diameter requires $\frac{1}{2}$ yard of 18-inch velvet. (This includes 2 inches for making.) If both sides of the brim are covered with velvet, allow twice this quantity, or 1 yard. One-half yard of 36-inch material is adequate in addition to the crown.

MATERIALS FOR HAT COVERINGS

Other types of brim coverings. Many hats are made with the top and underfacing of the brim in one piece by the use of a bias strip of the material. It is either folded through the center and stretched over the edge of the frame, or the material is held a little full on the edge and the fullness at the headsize is carelessly laid in folds or carefully plaited.

This type of brim may be made to look entirely different by means of a bias strip cut for both the top and the underfacing.

This method necessitates a few more inches, but it is more effective for contrasting materials without a nap or pile and it makes many interesting edge finishings possible. For this type of brim, measure at the widest point in the following manner: Place the end of tape measure close to the headsize on top of brim and carry it straight out over edge of brim and under, ending at the headsize. This gives twice the width of the brim, to which must be added $1\frac{1}{2}$ inches for making. Measure the circumference of the brim. If material is to be stretched plain over edge, do not allow extra for making, because of elasticity of bias strip.

Full or shirred brim. Measure circumference of brim and allow one and a fourth to one and a half times the circumference for velvets, duvetyns, or silks. Thin materials require more. Cut materials on the bias. In buying a strip of velvet, be sure that the estimate is sufficient (velvet is the only material sold on the bias). In the shops velvet is measured on the selvage, and a quarter of a yard makes a bias piece only 6 inches wide through the bias.

Velvet 22 inches wide makes a bias strip $29\frac{1}{3}$ inches long. If the circumference of the brim is not more than $29\frac{1}{3}$ inches, one width of 22-inch material is ample.

MEASURING FOR CROWNS

In estimating material for crowns, consider whether the crown is plain or draped. A crown made in one piece takes less material than other types. To estimate the quantity of material, measure from the base over the top to the base on the opposite side, from front to back. This gives the greatest diameter. For the average crown of this type $\frac{1}{2}$ yard of 18-inch material is sufficient.

Crown with plain tip and side band. Eighteen-inch material does not cut to good advantage for this type of crown because of the necessity of piecing when material is cut on the true bias. If the velvet is long enough to cut the band a little off the bias, the extra seam for piecing may be avoided. Suppose the tip measures 9 inches by 11 inches. This piece may be cut from a corner of the bias. The 22-inch width cuts to better advantage than the 18-inch. Measure for depth of side band as directed for brim. If band is to be covered plain, measure depth plus 2 inches. If a slight drape is desired, use one and one-half times the depth of band plus 2 inches for making.

For hats made with bias folds on the edge or a series of folds, the method of measuring is the same as for the brim in one piece. Observe that there are two sides to be covered and that the materials must be twice the greatest diameter. Measure bias strip through bias, not on selvage, when estimating quantity. To this quantity add material necessary for crown.

COVERING FRAME

Preparing frame for covering. In making hats of silk or satin, it is necessary to put on an extra covering of some kind to pad the frame. For this purpose, various materials may be used, such as cheesecloth, cotton crêpe, cotton wadding, mull, or outing flannel.

In cutting material for padding or covering for the hat it is more economical to make a pattern to fit the frame (see page 15, directions for copying shape in paper) than to cut the cloth free-hand according to directions given below. Place pattern thus made on material and cut, allowing margins for making ($\frac{1}{2}$ inch on the edge and for seams, and $\frac{3}{4}$ inch at headsize).

MATERIALS FOR HAT COVERINGS

Cut and fit the padding, following directions given for covering except that in this case it is overlapped at the joinings and not put in a seam. Likewise the edges need not be sewed, as the outside covering will hold the material in place.

Placing velvet on frame. To cover a sailor or slightly drooping brim by free-hand cutting proceed as follows: Mark center of brim from front to back. Place velvet on top side with lengthwise or warp thread on this line. If velvet has a laid pile, as in panne velvet or hatter's plush, place it so that the direction of the pile lies from back to front. Velvet appears richer when the observer looks into the pile. There is, however, some difference of opinion as to which way the pile should be. It may run from front to back or from side to side, or the bias may be placed at center front. One good rule to follow is to place the bias or corner of material at the part of brim most difficult to fit.

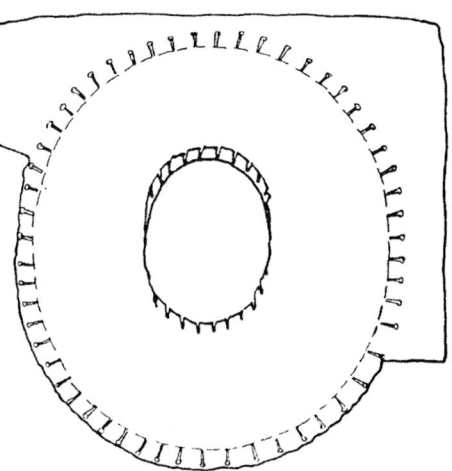

FIG. 42. *Stretching material on frame*

Begin to pin at front edge of brim, then back, right and left sides, sticking pins straight into edge of frame (Fig. 42). This method makes one pinhole only and does not mar the surface of the velvet or silk. In pinning velvet over brim, be sure that selvage extends beyond edge on both sides so that all or most of it can be removed. Trim velvet around edge of brim, allowing it to extend $\frac{1}{2}$ inch. Cut an oval piece from center of headsize, leaving $\frac{3}{4}$-inch margin around headsize. Slash at 1-inch intervals to within $\frac{1}{4}$ inch of headsize wire. Remove pins and stretch material gradually until it fits down over headsize band. Clip material again if necessary to make it fit well down on brim. Work very carefully, stretching and pinning so that material will fit snugly to headsize. If necessary, sew with stab stitches. Repin edge as follows: center front first, then center back, right and left sides, and halfway between each of these points. Continue pinning in this way until all fullness is worked out of edge. If material has stretched more than $\frac{1}{2}$ inch from edge, trim carefully to this width. Otherwise edge of frame will be bulky.

Sewing velvet to brim. Hold brim carefully between finger and thumb of left hand, taking out the pins as you sew. Place needle in hat just below cut edge of velvet. Take stitch in velvet about center of turned-over edge of velvet. In sewing around edge take great care not to pull material over underside, causing brim to assume a different shape. Be sure to avoid taking stitch too close to cut edge of material or a cord will be formed between stitches. The catstitch (page 91) or hemming may be used to fasten down this edge, but the catch stitch (page 91) draws fullness more evenly.

Facing brim. Place velvet on underside of brim, pinning from front to back, side to side, etc., with direction of pile the same as on top of brim. Stretch material, pinning to edges as on top brim. Pin two or three times at headsize, being careful to keep brim and material flat. If material is pushed into headsize, it will cause fullness at some part of brim, requiring a seam. If, on the other hand, material is stretched too tightly, it will cause the frame to be distorted.

Completing headsize. Cut a small oval from center of headsize, allowing $1\frac{1}{2}$-inch margin all around opening, and slash 1 inch apart. Turn these little slashed pieces up against band and sew them in place.

Preparing edge. Trim underfacing to within $\frac{1}{2}$ inch from edge of brim.

Finishing edge with wire. One of the best ways for finishing the edge of a plain covered hat is to sew in a piece of frame

MATERIALS FOR HAT COVERINGS

wire, lace wire, or cable cord. This gives a cord effect. Beginning at side back of frame, remove a few pins at a time and fold material over wire. Pin it if necessary to hold it in place. Repin material to edge of brim, placing pins just under wire to keep it from slipping down into frame. In turning material over wire, take care not to pull on the bias at the edge. Always work straight out from headsize to edge of brim to avoid fullness. Do not join wire until facing has been sewed to brim with slip stitches. Hold edge of brim between middle finger and thumb of left hand. Remove two or three pins at a time as the work proceeds. Place forefinger on wire, press down, and take a stitch into frame between facing of frame, forcing needle out under wire.

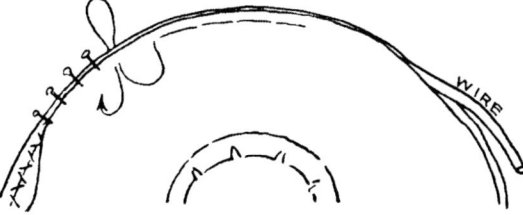

FIG. 43. *Finishing edge of brim. Tool material over wire*

With needle tuck material gently under wire, forming a cord. Be careful not to use force or to let material become loose. Take a stitch about $\frac{1}{4}$ inch long under the wire, and pass needle up between brim and facing. Draw thread tight to hold material around wire. Tool material as sewing proceeds (Fig. 43). (See Glossary.) Take a small stitch into the frame opposite where needle has come out, just catching material. Slant needle slightly coming back under wire in preparation for next stitch. Continue until finished. Cut wire so that it just meets and join it with a little clamp. (Metal clamps may be purchased in millinery shops.)

Or allow $\frac{1}{2}$-inch lap, straightening ends slightly. They need not be joined by tying, as the material will hold them in place. Overlapping is not satisfactory because of bulkiness, and there is danger that the ends of the wire will make holes in the material. Velvets and other pile fabrics are sometimes slip-stitched on the edge instead of being given the cord effect.

If a soft effect is desired on the edge of the hat, such as folds, shirrings, or plaitings extending from brim, they must be added before the underfacing is attached.

COVERING IRREGULAR SHAPES

For this type remember the rule of placing the bias or corner of velvet on the most difficult part of the frame first. Determine location of seam before cutting material. It may be placed at back or where it will show least. Pin material into irregular part of frame on upper part of brim. At center front of headsize cut material about 2 inches from headline and 2 or 3 inches on each side of this point, curving to follow headline. Slash from this cut line toward headsize two or three times, just enough to allow material to fit over headsize band and into frame. Remove pins from headline and edge of brim and pull the material. Refit and pin to same place. Then arrange material around brim, placing all fullness where seam will be. Continue to cut about 2 inches from headsize line, a little at a time, slashing toward headsize and pinning material in place. The material must be stretched until it is perfectly even, and it must follow the line of the brim. Pin material together for seam. Cut around edge of brim and at seam, allowing $\frac{3}{4}$-inch margin.

Joining seam. Mark frame and material front, back, and sides. Be sure to mark seam. It is advisable to remove part, if not all, of velvet to join seam, by machine or small stitches by hand. Machine stitching is preferred. Steam velvet, pressing seam open with fingers. Press other materials with an iron.

Gluing to frame. If milliners' glue can be obtained, put it on the frame in decided curves of the hat. If material is to be turned over edge and sewed to underside, spread glue all over top of brim. If underfacing is put on first, so that edge finish is on top side, place glue carefully about 1 inch from edge to permit material to be turned over wire. It is advisable not to use glue for silk or satin hats, as it is likely to spot material.

MATERIALS FOR HAT COVERINGS

Instead, fasten material to frame with tiny invisible stitches. The material may be put on without stitches or glue to hold it into the lines of the hat. This gives a softer effect to brim.

Replacing covering on brim. To replace material after sewing seam, work from front to back and side to side, placing and pinning markings together. Draw fullness gradually from headsize to the curve in the brim, then to edge. If material has been carefully fitted and marked, it is easy to replace. Retrim margin $\frac{1}{2}$ inch from edge and catch-stitch material to underside as for plain sailor.

Underfacing irregular shapes. Place velvet so that the pile runs in the same direction as that on top. Pin center front first, then to headsize, keeping material smooth on outer edge. All fullness must be worked from edge of brim to headsize. Work material around brim from each side of front until it is smooth. Pin together at seam and cut material, allowing $\frac{3}{4}$ inch.

Cut material around headsize, leaving about a 2-inch margin. Remove some of the pins from edge of brim and turn facing back. Mark seam, turn, and sew facing together, then steam and press it. If it is necessary to remove entire facing to sew seam, carefully mark both pieces, brim and material, so that the two can be matched and put together again.

Pin and finish edge as for a plain sailor. Slash material at headsize just enough to turn it over headband, and sew it in place.

Make crown and sew it to brim. (See "Crowns.")

Making hats of one material. From time to time it is fashionable to make hats from one material. There is the flower hat, usually a toque entirely covered with roses, violets, leaves, or any flat, soft kind of flowers. The bird hat is covered partially or entirely with the breasts of birds. Hats may be made of fur. Mole, ermine, squirrel, sealskin, Persian lamb, and mink are well adapted to making small toques or turbans. Leather hats are serviceable for sports wear and rainy weather. Hats made entirely of lace or ribbon usually have brims.

CHAPTER VIII

COVERING CROWNS

> Crown Drawn Tightly over Foundation
> Plain Crown in Two Pieces: Cutting Tip—Covering Tip—Cutting Side Band
> Soft Crown No. 1
> Soft Crown No. 2: Tip—Side Band
> Sectional Crown
> Attaching Brim to Crown
> Finishing at Base with Cord

Several methods have been given, in a previous chapter, for making crown frames. These instructions may be applied to both the foundation and the outside covering. Directions for additional styles of crowns are given here.

CROWN DRAWN TIGHTLY OVER FOUNDATION

Use the method given for molding a crown over a block. In this case stretch covering over frame. Velvets and malines may be steamed. Place material straight over crown from front to back. If hat is made of velvet, take care to have the direction of the pile the same in both crown and brim. The two general methods of placing material on the crown are: (1) Keep front, back, and sides plain, working all fullness into tiny groups at bias corners of material. This causes fullness to form at four places on crown. (2) Form small plaits all around the crown. Pin fullness carefully in place, then turn cut edge of goods down over edge of crown, and catch it with small, invisible stitches. This method of crown finishing necessitates some form of trimming at the base, which may be a small bias fold of the same material or a band of ribbon.

COVERING CROWNS 79

PLAIN CROWN IN TWO PIECES

When the crown is made in two pieces (top or "tip" and side band), a variety of effects may be obtained. If the top is separated from the side band by a sharp edge, as in the usual sailor crown, the sharp edge separating the two is the natural division line. The two pieces may be joined by a covered wire cord, giving a cord effect. If top of crown has a gradual slope, top and side band may be placed at any division line. In other words, the top may extend down the side of the crown any depth, or the side band may run up on the top.

Cutting tip. Cut crown tip so that the direction of the pile will be same as in the brim. The tip must be cut with sufficient margin to sew to side band (at least 1 inch larger).

Covering tip. Pin material to frame from front to back, side to side, forming quarters, then eighths, and so on until all fullness is stretched out of tip. Fullness may be removed easily if care is taken to stretch material on the bias, pulling from straight of goods to bias. Sew material on desired line for edge of tip with a straight row of backstitches about $\frac{1}{2}$ inch in length (Fig. 44). Stretch material while sewing, as this helps to remove fullness. Steam tip so as to get a more finished effect.

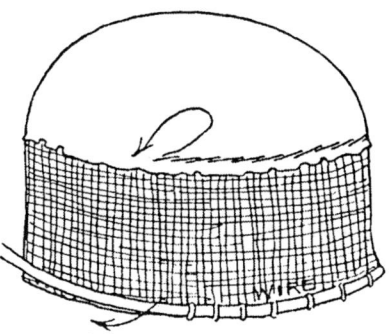

FIG. 44. *Covering tip*

Cutting side band. If side band is straight or only slightly curved, use bias band. Measure depth of side band and cut material 2 inches wider for making. One-half inch is needed for turning on each edge, because the goods will become an inch narrower in stretching around crown. Pin bias strip to sideband foundation and stretch it around crown so that both sides fit smoothly. Pin joinings together at selvage or warp edge. Remove bias strip from band. Stitch seam by machine. For napped or pile material, as duvetyn or velvet, steam the seam open. For other fabrics press it with an iron.

Another method of making this band is to pin bias material around crown before cutting. Be sure that material fits smoothly top and bottom. Pin seams. Trim both sides of band, allowing ½-inch margin. Take band off and stitch it. Join side band on bias (along selvage) or make seam straight. (The latter will make a straight line from top to base of crown.) Replace material to side band, noting desirable place for seam. Shape of hat and trimming to be used will determine location of seam. Pin material in a few places, top and bottom.

Finish top and base of side band with frame wire, lace wire, or cable cord as for edge of brim. Sew top of side band first. Pin material over wire or cord and attach it to crown. With stab stitch sew through and back again just under wire, giving a cord effect (Fig. 45). There are three choices for joining wire: (1) Connect wire joinings with clamps made for the purpose. (2) Let one overlap the other, which makes a bulky joining. (3) Cut wires so they will just meet.

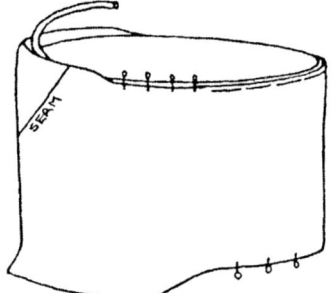

FIG. 45. *Joining side band and tip. Turning and sewing material over wire to give cord effect*

(This requires unusual care). Turn lower edge of material over crown base and catch it in place, or pin material over a wire and attach it to brim, causing wire to give a cord effect at base of crown.

SOFT CROWN NO. 1

This style of crown is made in two pieces, tip and side band. The size depends upon the effect desired and the foundation crown to be covered. Cut tip and side band as follows: Regular oval tip 7½ inches by 9½ inches (note direction of pile fabrics). Cut bias side band 8½ inches wide (or one and one-half times depth of side band) and 26½ inches long. Sew band together,

COVERING CROWNS

steam or press it open. Pin band to tip, placing right sides together, and sew it in place.

Cord covered with a bias fold of material is often sewed between band and tip. In this case the cord is sewed to tip first, then band is attached to the two. Turn band and pin it to crown frame, draping sides as desired. To keep folds from losing their shape it is sometimes advisable to line side band with piece of thin muslin, light outing flannel, or tarlatan. A molded crown of crinoline is often used for the foundation.

SOFT CROWN NO. 2

Tip. Cut an ellipse 5 by $6\frac{1}{2}$ inches. Pin this to top of crown frame and sew in place $\frac{1}{4}$ inch from edge.

Side band. Measure width of side band by placing tape measure on sewing line of ellipse attached to frame, then measure straight down to base of crown and add 2 inches. This dimension gives width of band, and measures approximately 8 inches through the bias and $26\frac{1}{2}$ inches long. Sew the two ends together. (Vary width of material for crowns of different heights.)

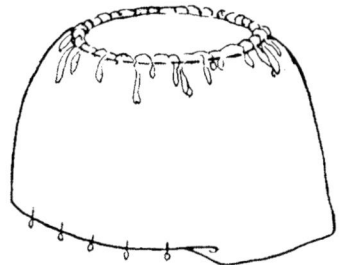

FIG. 46. *Combination of plain side band and full and plain tip*

Cut wire or cord 14 inches long and join ends, making a circle. Sew one side of material over wire, giving shirred effect. Bend circle, making an oval. Pin this oval over piece sewed to top of crown; pin, and sew in place. Bottom edge may be finished in any desired style. This crown gives the effect of plain side band and a combination of full and plain tip (Fig. 46).

This style of side band may be used for a one-piece crown. Measure from center of tip to base. Use this dimension for depth of crown, add 2 inches for making. The distance around the crown is the same as above. Sew seam on bias. Put several rows of gatherings on one edge. Draw up threads and place right sides together and sew, forming a seam $1\frac{1}{2}$ to 2 inches. Place this shirred piece over the crown and pin. Draw up gathering threads to fit tip and fasten in place. Finish crown at base.

SECTIONAL CROWN

Cut center line of each section on same thread of material. That is, if one section is cut bias, the others should be cut in the same manner. If material is plaid or checked, match sections.

Make this crown without a foundation frame. In some cases it is preferable to line each piece with thin muslin or crinoline before making. Finish seams plain, stitch, or use a cord covered with a bias fold of material. The seams may be made a little more decorative by sewing them on the outside and binding each one.

ATTACHING BRIM TO CROWN

Pin crown to brim in four places: front, back, right and left sides. Try on frame to adjust crown.

Slip-stitch crown to brim by first placing needle inside crown, then stick through to outside near base of crown. Pull thread slightly, making a larger hole in material; put needle back into this hole (being careful not to catch threads of material), slant slightly, then stick straight through to the underside of brim. Repeat in the same manner from underside to top, sewing around the crown. By this method, crown may be attached to brim without showing stitches on right side.

FINISHING AT BASE WITH CORD

If a wire is used to make a cord finish, first tie-tack crown to brim in about four places. Fold outside covering back, place needle through crown near base and straight to underside, then back again as suggested above, only in this case tie the two ends of thread on top. Fold material over wire and pin it to base of crown. Sew in place by using slip stitch for underside of brim; and for top the same stitch used for edge of brim, giving a cord finish.

CHAPTER IX

COVERING HAT WITH BRAIDS

SEWING BRAIDS

PREPARATION OF BRAIDS

FRAMES FOR BRAIDS

COVERING BRIM: Underfacing with Braid—Bindings, Silk and Velvet—Extending Braid from Edge—Combining Silk and Braid—Covering Brim with Plaque

MAKING CROWNS: Draped Crown—Tam-o'-Shanter Crown—Sectional Crown—Braids Going across Crown

SEWING BRAIDS OVER WIRE MOLD

REMOVING BRIM FROM MOLD

SEWING BRAIDS

Examine the braid to see if there is a right and wrong side. Begin with the end that will permit sewing from right to left. Hold the hat in front of worker so that the brim is in an upright position. Avoid letting the brim touch the lap, which might bend the shape. Sew with braid toward worker. The side of brim to be covered depends somewhat on the combination of materials and the style of hat. When possible, cover upper side first, leaving underfacing for the last. For sewing braids together, use cotton thread of same color. Silk thread tends to slip.

Some braids are pliable and easy to work with, while others are very stiff and difficult to handle. In the more pliant braids, often a thread or series of threads is found on one side. One or several of these threads may be drawn up to fit the hat before the other rows are fastened to this one. Never overlap the braids more than is necessary when sewing one row to another around the brim, because this only makes the hat heavy and uses an unnecessary quantity of braid. The plain woven braids need not be cut as they meet each time around the hat. In case braid is very wide, or if it has a pattern that would be improved by being cut for each row, cut it.

In covering brim with braid, inner edges of each row continue to have a greater amount of fullness as brim nears completion. Draw up threads and sew row in place. See "Sports Hats" for covering irregular shapes.

For some nontransparent braids it is advisable to cover the frame with inexpensive material the color of the braid. This prevents the light frame from showing through. In making a hat of silk on one side and braid on the other, it depends upon the pliability of braid which side should be covered first. If possible, sew braid on one side before silk is attached to opposite side. In some cases silk may be put on first and the braid slip-stitched to the opposite side.

PREPARATION OF BRAIDS

Before sewing the stiff or some of the rough braids, place the braid in folds of wet paper about two hours to make it pliable. In the process of making, leave the braid folded in paper, removing just enough to work with. This method keeps stiff braids pliable and rough braids less brittle.

Another method of dampening braid is to place it in water a few yards at a time. This causes braid to be very wet, making it difficult to handle until it is slightly dried.

FRAMES FOR BRAIDS

The same foundation frames that were used for making fabric hats may be applied to the braid hat. The number of ways for making are just as varied. Transparent braids may be made over a wire frame. For the soft hat without a frame sew the braid over a wire mold made for that purpose. If braid has been dampened, lacquer it to restore its finish before removing it from the frame. Lacquer gives added stiffness.

COVERING BRIM

Before sewing braid to the brim, consider various methods for finishing the edge. The pattern of braid will guide somewhat in the choice of finish for the edge.

If braid has a scallop, or some other form of decoration on one side, and if top of brim is to be covered first, begin at center back of hat so as to work from right to left. Turn end of braid under, and fold it over edge of hat with scallop side of braid folded under

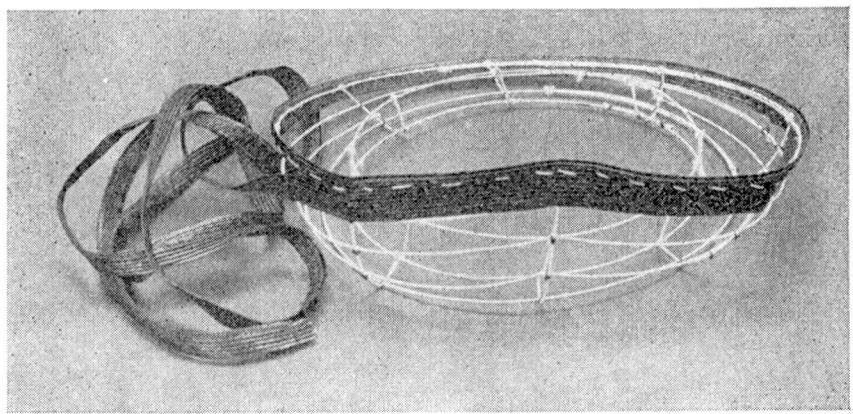

FIG. 47. *Molding braid brim over wire frame*

brim. With stab stitch sew through and back again near the two edges. Where the two ends meet, overlap them about 1 inch. Do not cut braid, but gradually slant scalloped edge from underside, bringing it to top and to lower edge of braid. Overlap the two slightly and continue to sew the rows around brim until it is covered (Fig. 47). For irregular brim, see "Sports Hats." Or sew braid over edge as directed above, but instead of continuing to cover in one piece cut braid, allowing $\frac{1}{2}$ inch to turn under. Place the two folded ends so that they just meet, and sew them in place carefully. The next row of braid may be placed even with the edge or any distance from it. Avoid too much overlapping, as it will waste material and make a heavy hat.

Underfacing with braid. Stretch braid and pin it in the same manner as for the top. In sewing with stab stitch, slant needle each time a stitch is taken through hat. Hide stitches by placing needle under mesh of braid. Facings of various materials are often used. Follow directions for covering hats with velvet, pages 73 f., or see "Sports Hats."

Bindings, silk and velvet. See previous instructions for cutting bias folds and edge finishings. Choose either method for edge finish. Braids may be put on in the regulation way or a plaque may be cut and stretched in place.

Extending braid from edge. The hat may be enlarged by extending braid beyond edge of brim. Examples: tuscan, horse hair, or pyroxylin. The braid may continue in a spiral or it may be cut each time around.

Combining silk and braid. Pin first row of braid even with edge of brim, but do not sew it in place. Then stretch second row in place. (See above instructions.)

Cover opposite side with silk, following previous instructions. Unpin braid at edge and catch-stitch silk to frame under braid. Slip-stitch edge of braid to silk.

Or, pin silk in place first and catch-stitch it to edge of frame. If braid is sufficiently pliable to attach without sewing through frame, slip-stitch it in place.

Covering brim with plaque. Stretch edge of plaque around edge of brim and cut or rip plaque at headsize, adding about 1 inch to turn into opening. To join braid down center back, cut it about 2 inches larger. Rip each braid section about 1 inch, then dovetail or interlace one edge over the other and sew it in place. This gives a good finish for a plaque when it is necessary to make a seam. If the plaque is larger than size of brim, rip a few rows from outer edge to place on the facing or top of brim. For the unfinished space, silk, maline, or georgette may be used. The small circle cut from headsize may be used for tip of crown.

Side band may be finished with material used for brim.

COVERING HAT WITH BRAIDS

MAKING CROWNS

Use the same methods for stretching and pinning braids on crown as for brim. Sew either in a spiral or by joining each row around to correspond with brim.

Begin either at base or at tip, depending upon the effect desired. In working from *base* to *tip* the braids will overlap (Fig.

FIG. 48. *Molding braid crown over wire frame*

48). In working from *tip* to *base* the braids will underlap. Both ways are correct. Preference is given to the former for plain crowns.

Begin at base of back, extending braid a little below edge. Overlap as little as possible and stretch lower edge slightly. If there is much fullness at the inner edge, draw up threads until braid is shape of crown. If there are no threads to draw, use a basting for this purpose. Finish center of top by turning end of braid under and slip it underneath last row before sewing it down. Tack well and press it lightly with an iron.

In making crowns of fancy braid, cut braid each time around crown, turning under each end so that folded edges just meet. Sew as directed for binding edge of brim.

Draped crown. Make flat button or rosette of braid, twist the end under, and sew it in place. Hold each succeeding row a little easy by drawing threads and overlapping braid about $\frac{1}{8}$ inch on underside. With small stitches sew through and back again near edge of braid, being careful to hide stitches in weave of braid on top. Form round flat piece or oval shape until it is large enough for top of crown or frame to be draped; then gradually draw in each row of braid, forming a hood or basket. Take care to draw braid with an even tension. When hood is finished, press it on the wrong side. Pin it to top of crown and drape it around in irregular folds. Pin all in place before tacking. This hood may be made to come to the edge of the brim so as to give the effect of a hat in one piece, provided the lower edge of the hood is about the size of the edge of the brim. The size of hood when finished depends on the size of crown and style of hat to be made.

Tam-o'-shanter crown. Make a large plaque by beginning at the center, as for a draped crown. Take care to keep edges from being full. Since the beauty of this crown is in its perfect flatness, place it on the table frequently to see that it is flat. The size to be made depends on size of crown, as this plaque must be large enough to fit over the crown to the base all around. Before tacking the crown to the frame, press it on the wrong side with a warm iron. Divide it in half, then in quarters, and plait it to lower edge of crown after crown has been tacked to brim.

Sectional crown. Braids are put on also by dividing the crown into quarters. Begin at lower edge or base of crown, work to center of tip, turn braid so as to make a decided point, and let braid go to base of crown again. Outline quarters first, then gradually fill in quarters until entire crown is covered. In turning corners, take care to keep a perfect line from side to side. Each row of braid must be cut $\frac{1}{2}$ inch below base so it can be turned over wire as quarters are filled.

COVERING HAT WITH BRAIDS

Braids going across crown. Begin at base of center crown, extending braid $\frac{1}{2}$ inch from base, and let braid continue to base on opposite side, working from front to back. Cut each successive row as it is put on the crown, overlapping the ends about $\frac{1}{8}$ inch. Finish one side, then the other. Turn edge under around base of crown and sew it to brim. Braids may be sewed to a wire mold for this purpose. Take care not to catch the wires. If necessary, lacquer the crown to restore gloss or stiffness before removing it from the frame. Transparent crowns may be made over a block. Pin braid in place, remove it from block, and sew. Then replace it on the block and press it into shape.

SEWING BRAIDS OVER WIRE MOLD

Any type of braid may be sewed over a wire mold. Consider first whether braid is pliable enough to handle without moistening. Liséré braid has been used for the model illustrated (Fig. 48). It was placed between folds of wet newspaper about two hours before being sewed.

It is desirable to remove only the necessary quantity of braid from the paper at a time. Begin at center or near center back and sew braid to edge wire with heavy white thread (on black braid). Extend braid slightly from edge wire and sew it in place securely. Place second row, overlapping the edges slightly, and sew with stab stitch, using medium-weight black mercerized thread. Be careful not to catch stitches around wire. Do not draw braid tight in sewing it around brim, because it leaves an outline of spoke wires on finished brim. As brim nears completion, instead of stab stitch use a form of slip stitch, keeping needle on right side. Instead of allowing needle to go to wrong side, keep within meshes of braid. At headsize be careful to sew braid well up on headline. Any stitch may be used that is easy for the worker. The model shown in Fig. 47 has an irregular outline and requires short lengths of braid to fill in the space left near the headsize.

REMOVING BRIM FROM MOLD

Clip white stitches and gradually remove brim from mold. On inside of frame, with stab stitch, sew a piece of braid even with edge of brim. Short stitches must be taken on both sides; slant the needle to obtain space between stitches. To fasten ends of braid leave about 2 inches for overlap. For a distance of about 1 inch on each end rip machine stitching from braid and dovetail or interlock ends and tack them in place. If braid has been moistened and the luster lost, enamel or lacquer the hat on both sides of brim to restore finish. If brim seems too stiff, steam it slightly. If enamel or lacquer cannot be obtained, any hat dye may be used.

The crown should be pressed and lacquered before it is removed from the mold. Attach brim and crown. See instructions for joining crown to brim, page 82.

CHAPTER X

STITCHES AND PROCESSES USED IN CONSTRUCTION OF HATS

STITCHES: Backstitch—Catch Stitch—Catstitch—Hemming Stitch—Lacing Stitch—Running or Gathering Stitch—Simulated Fold—Slip Hemming—Slip Stitch—Stab Stitch—Swinging Tack—Tie Tack—Wire Stitch

Backstitch. Used for joining velvets or any other materials which need close sewing. A long backstitch is used for fastening covering on the edge of the brim if it is to be covered with a fold; and for sewing material of the tip to the side crown, as in Figure 44, on page 79.

FIG. 49. *Backstitch*

Work from right to left. Take a long stitch forward and a short stitch back, causing stitches to overlap similar to outline stitch (Fig. 49). This is unlike ordinary backstitch which, on the right side, imitates machine stitching.

Catch stitch. Differs from catstitch in that there is no crossing of the thread. This is the least conspicuous stitch for fastening hems and folds. Turn material to the wrong side and sew from right to left. Slip needle under fold for first stitch, take second stitch just below

FIG. 50. *Catch stitch*

cut edge of fold. Take care to catch only one or two threads or part of a thread on the back of the goods. Alternate from side to side, taking tiny parallel stitches (Fig. 50).

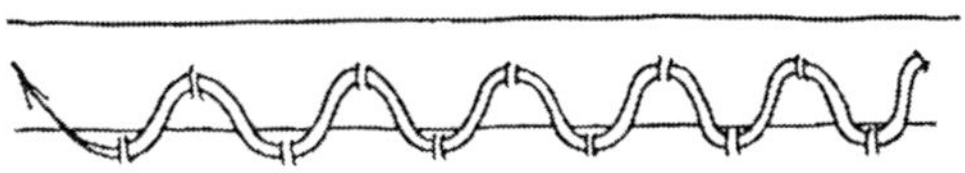

Catstitch. So named because it crosses like a cat's front paws (Fig. 51). It is generally used for attaching material to the frame and for hemming folds.

92 HATS AND HOW TO MAKE THEM

Sew from left to right, taking up a small stitch with the needle. Make both rows of stitches parallel, crossing the thread between. (Sometimes called herringbone.) See catch stitch.

FIG. 51. *Catstitch*

Hemming stitch. Used for fastening down the selvage edge of ribbon on a wire or for hemming silks for trimming. Work from right to left on edge of folded hem. Take a small stitch in material at edge of folded hem-line and point needle so that a tiny stitch catches folded edge. Take next stitch a little to the left of the last stitch.

Lacing stitch. May be used for drawing the two edges together in making flat folds. Make stitches $\frac{1}{4}$ inch apart, placing needle for each stitch about $\frac{1}{8}$ inch under cut edge. (See page 97, "Flat Folds.")

Running or gathering stitch. Used for joining materials and for shirrings.

Simulated fold. This fold is used in preparing trimmings. It finishes edges without applying an extra piece of material.

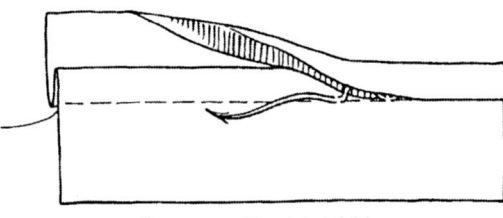

FIG. 52. *Simulated fold*

Bows may be made from any kind of fabric, with this fold used as a decoration. It is particularly effective on mourning hats because they are often self-trimmed. To make a $\frac{1}{4}$-inch fold a 1-inch allowance is required. Turn 1 inch of the material to the right side, pin, and baste it along folded edge. Then make a line of running stitches along folded edge forming a tiny tuck not more than $\frac{1}{4}$ inch wide. Turn cut edge of material and slip-stitch it to running stitches, hiding the little tuck within (Fig. 52).

Slip hemming. Similar to the slip stitch (Fig. 53). Used in making rolled hems.

STITCHES AND PROCESSES USED

Slip stitch. Used on trimmings and bias folds and for all parts requiring invisible joining; as, for example, the two pieces covering both sides of the hat brim. Place needle near edge (not on edge) of material, just catching the side that is turned under. Bring needle out and catch opposite side, by beginning the stitch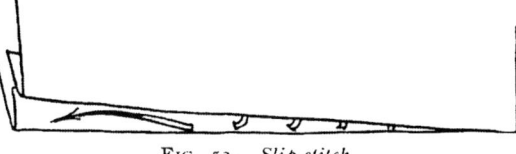

FIG. 53. *Slip stitch*

just opposite where the last stitch ended. Take care not to let the stitches show. They must be made close together around the edge of the brim (Fig. 53).

Stab stitch. Used to sew wire around headsize, to fasten trimmings in place, to attach bias folds of cambric or crinoline to edge of brim, and to attach brim to crown. Wherever it is necessary to take one stitch at a time, use the stab stitch. Push needle through and back again each time a stitch is needed.

Swinging tack. Used where trimming must hang loose from hat; as, for example, a plume. Take two or three stitches connecting the two surfaces. Leave space desired by allowing

FIG. 54. *Tie tack*

threads to be loose. Wind thread around loops thus made. Fasten end of thread.

Tie tack. Used wherever it is necessary to fasten trimming invisibly. Take a single stitch through material and tie the ends of the thread (Fig. 54), having a knot in one end for convenience.

Wire stitch. (Sometimes called tailor's buttonhole stitch.) Fasten thread by using a knot or by taking two or three stitches one over the other. Place wire on edge of frame, holding it in place with thumb and finger of left hand. Take a stitch through the frame near or just under the wire to left of knot and pull thread through until a small loop remains, then pass needle through this loop from back to front and draw thread tight.

FIG. 55. *Wire stitch*

This completes one stitch. Space stitches $\frac{3}{8}$ inch or more apart (Fig. 55).

The blanket stitch is sometimes confused with the wire stitch, but it does not hold so well; neither does overhanding take the place of the wire stitch. The buttonhole stitch is sometimes used and is very satisfactory.

CHAPTER XI

EDGE FINISHES AND BINDINGS

BIAS FOLDS: Cutting the Bias—Stitching through Thin Materials—Joining Bias Pieces
FLAT FOLDS
FRENCH OR MILLINER'S FOLD
BIAS FOLD ON EDGE OF BRIM: Estimating Width of Fold—Stretching Fold on Edge of Brim—Placing Seams—Replacing on Brim—Finishing Fold
FOLD ON EDGE OF BRIM WITHOUT A WIRE
FOLD MADE BEFORE ATTACHING
NARROW RIBBON OR BRAID BINDING ON EDGE
NARROW BINDINGS OF SILK OR ORGANDY
COMBINATION OF BRIM COVERING AND BINDING
PLAIN BIAS FOLD EXTENDING BEYOND EDGE OF BRIM
PLAIN EDGE: Drooping—Upturning—Maline Folds
SHIRRED EDGES: Methods No. 1, No. 2, No. 3
SECTIONAL FACINGS
CORD FINISHING: Two Methods—Splicing Cord

BIAS FOLDS

A bias fold on the edge of a hat is sometimes called a flange. In this book the word *flange* will not be used, but it is understood that *flange* and *bias fold* give practically the same meaning. The definition of the word *flange* is a "projecting flat rim." This is confusing to the amateur because the bias folds and their applications are not always flat. The bias fold is made to produce many different effects by combinations of texture and contrasting colors. With one exception all materials used for making folds and edge finishings are more effective when cut on a true bias. Maline is the exception. It is cut lengthwise.

Cutting the bias. Fold material at right angles so that warp and filling threads are parallel. When folded this way the cut

96 HATS AND HOW TO MAKE THEM

end of material, if perfectly straight, will be parallel to the selvage. Cut through fold to obtain a true bias. In measuring width of bias do not measure along selvage or straight edge, but across bias at right angles to folded bias edge. Fold material, pin it in place, and cut (Fig. 56).

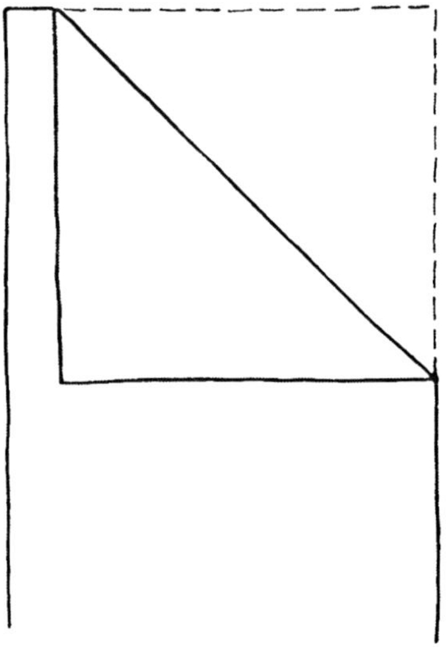

To cut chiffons, georgettes, silks, and other thin materials, the following method is recommended. Take a piece of paper having a right-angle corner. From this corner measure out on each side of paper an equal distance. Connect these points. Measure at right angles to this line the widths of bias desired and draw parallel lines. Pin or baste paper on material, being sure to have it even. Cut through drawn lines. This insures a true bias and even cutting.

FIG. 56. *Folding material for bias fold*

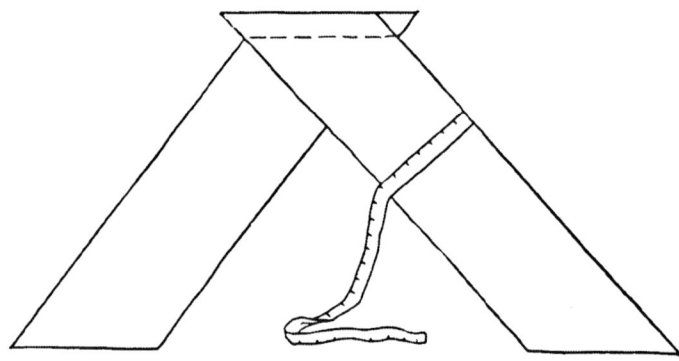

FIG. 57. *Measuring and joining bias fold*

Stitching through thin materials. Thin silks, crêpes, and chiffons tend to pucker when stitched by machine. To avoid

EDGE FINISHES AND BINDING

this place a piece of paper beneath material and stitch through both. Tear paper away when stitching is finished and press seam.

Joining bias pieces. Make seam on a true bias, following warp threads or line of selvage. Cut off selvage. Slip one piece past the other the depth of seam, pin them together, and stitch (Fig. 57, page 96.) Steam the seams open or press them with an iron. Carefully note the direction of the pile in working with velvet. The material will determine which method of pressing is desirable. When joining bias strips for circular trimmings, be sure to join seams along straight edge of material and not at right angles to bias edge.

FLAT FOLDS

Cut folds twice the width desired when finished. Turn both edges over to wrong side until they meet in center of fold. With

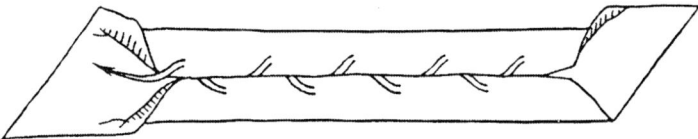

FIG. 58. *Flat fold*

lacing stitch (page 92) draw edges together by placing needle under material $\frac{1}{8}$ inch from edge and take stitches $\frac{1}{4}$ inch apart (Fig. 58). Draw the two edges together, giving the same effect as lacing a shoe with one string.

FRENCH OR MILLINER'S FOLD

The width required is two and one-half times the width desired when finished, plus $\frac{1}{4}$ inch for making. Turn top edge down the depth it is to be when finished. Turn bottom cut edge up $\frac{1}{4}$ inch, and turn again to within $\frac{1}{4}$ inch from top edge of fold (Fig. 59, page 98). Secure with a slip-stitch catching to back. Be careful not to let stitches show through on the right side. The French or milliner's fold is commonly used for finishing the base of the crown after it has been attached to the brim.

It is used also for decorating any part of the brim. Fasten the fold with a slip stitch. In placing either a flat or a milliner's fold on base of crown, pin one end in position and stretch it around crown. Pin the two together and sew. Finish with a small tailored bow or with trimming. The milliner's fold may be made on the crown without sewing. Fold one end as directed for making. Pin it to crown, then fold and gradually stretch it, pinning it in place and keeping material snug at the base.

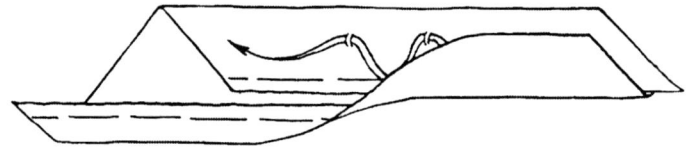

FIG. 59. *Milliner's fold*

Sew joinings together and finish as above. If this fold has been carefully stretched, and the strip is cut wide enough to keep edge folded inside, it will be necessary to tack it only once or twice.

BIAS FOLD ON EDGE OF BRIM

Estimating width of fold. For a plain fold that is to be stretched on edge of brim, it is a safe, though rough, estimate to take twice the width of fold plus $1\frac{1}{2}$ inches for making. The 1 inch is allowed for turning under on each side and the $\frac{1}{2}$ inch is for stretching. Some materials, such as georgette, crêpe, and organdy, have greater elasticity than velvet. For these materials, it is best to stretch a few inches of material over the brim so that allowance for stretching can be approximated. In using any of the above thin materials it is advisable to double the fold or use a lining of some kind. Example: two pieces of organdy; or one of georgette crêpe and two of cotton crêpe.

Stretching fold on edge of brim. For a velvet fold 1 inch finished on both sides of brim, cut material $3\frac{1}{2}$ inches wide. Fold strip through middle, place it over edge of brim. Stick a pin

EDGE FINISHES AND BINDING

straight through both fold and brim. Stretch material through center of fold until all fullness is out of inner edge. Stick two or three pins through edge to hold fold in place while working around brim. At the joining, pin ends together. Note carefully direction of bias and put pins in the two pieces, marking place for seam and direction for cutting bias strip. Allow $\frac{1}{4}$-inch seam. Take bias strip from brim and stitch seam (Fig. 62, page 103). Press or steam seam as directed.

Placing seams. In replacing bias band to edge of brim, note position of seams. If there is one seam only, place it near back or side back; if there are two seams, place them at sides. If the strip needs a small piecing, do not have seams too near together.

Replacing on brim. Begin at one seam on fold. Pin center over edge and stretch it in place as directed above. Be careful not to have fold too tight or brim will tend to draw out of shape. On the other hand, if it is too loose it will not make a good finish.

Finishing fold. Turn $\frac{1}{2}$ inch of material over a wire or cord and sew it to brim with the usual slip stitch, making a cord finish. (For tooling the edge, see "Finishing Edge with Wire," page 74.)

FOLD ON EDGE OF BRIM WITHOUT A WIRE

Pin, stitch, and join fold as in previous work. Turn material under on both sides $\frac{1}{2}$ inch, pin it in place, and slip-stitch it to brim. Take a stitch under fold near edge. Take second stitch directly opposite into material on brim. Repeat in same manner, causing length of stitch to alternate, first into fold, then to brim. Note that a stitch must begin opposite where last stitch ended.

FOLD MADE BEFORE ATTACHING

To measure fold, follow previous instructions for fitting fold. Turn edge over to wrong side $\frac{1}{2}$ inch, catch-stitch as directed for edge of brim. Replace fold on edge of brim according to the directions given, page 99. If fold is well stretched, it will not be necessary to slip-stitch the two together. If extra sewing is necessary, make long slip stitches. One side of this fold can be finished with a wire and the other side catch-stitched and not fastened to the hat. This is possible only when the fold is very tightly stretched.

NARROW RIBBON OR BRAID BINDING ON EDGE

For a narrow edge finish ribbons and braids are commonly used. They must measure twice the finished width desired. Starting at back, pin material over edge of brim and sew it with stab stitch, catching both sides together. Join ribbon by turning one end under and lapping it a sufficient depth over the other end. Sew it in place. Braid may be joined in the same way. Or, turn each end under and allow folded edges just to meet.

NARROW BINDINGS OF SILK OR ORGANDY

Cut silk or organdy four times the width of the bias plus $\frac{1}{4}$ inch for making and $\frac{1}{4}$ inch for stretching. Fold strip through middle, pin it together, making one side a fold and the other a cut edge. Place cut edges of fold on top of brim, even with edge. Stretch fold around brim until fullness is out of folded edge. Mark direction of bias for joinings, letting the edges just meet. Remove fold, open strip, and join it on bias. Press seams, refold strip, and replace it on brim. Stretch and pin fold, placing seams nearer back than front, and proceed as above. Backstitch the two about $\frac{1}{4}$ inch from edge of brim. Turn this fold over to underside, giving a soft finish. It is not always necessary to sew fold when it is turned over. This method of binding is very good for taffetas, satins, georgette crêpes, and organdies. It gives the effect of a narrow binding on one side of the brim and a wider binding on the opposite side. With heavier material use similar method. Cut twice the finished width plus extra quantity for making.

EDGE FINISHES AND BINDING

COMBINATION OF BRIM COVERING AND BINDING

Cut strip on bias the width of brim and add an additional quantity for making. Pin and stretch strip around brim. Remove it from brim and sew it. Replace it, putting the two right sides together, and backstitch cut edge to edge of brim. Turn this piece to opposite side, being careful to keep an even line for binding around edge. Fasten material to headsize in plaits or gathers. If there is a decided curve in the brim, material must be caught in place at this point before it is attached to headsize. The reverse side of brim must be covered before the combination of binding and facing is put on.

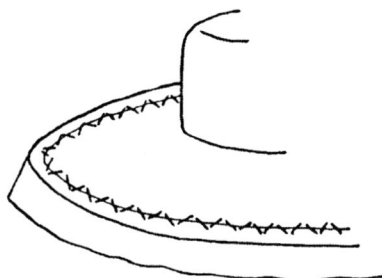

FIG. 60. *Bias fold drooping and extending from brim*

PLAIN BIAS FOLD EXTENDING BEYOND EDGE OF BRIM

Cut a strip twice the width of finished fold plus ½ inch for making. The length depends upon the size of the hat. Cover top of hat as directed for plain covering and catch-stitch to under edge of brim. Pin fold to edge, holding just enough fullness to keep outer edge plain. Pin joinings together in order to mark carefully the place for cutting on the bias. Remove a part, if not all, of fold, open, stitch, and press seam. Replace fold on hat, noting placing of seams as directed. Baste fold in place (Fig. 60). Put on underfacing, following previous instructions. Finish with a wire. Underfacing is attached in same way as top facing (Fig. 61). (See "Finishing Edge with Wire," page 74.)

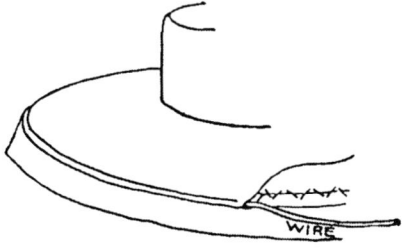

FIG. 61. *Covering top of brim*

PLAIN EDGE

Use above method for either of the folds. For this style of fold put material on without fullness, causing fold to cup. That is, it will droop from the edge of the hat, or it will stand up, giving a different effect. The difference in making is in the brim covering.

Drooping. Put underfacing on first and catch-stitch it to top edge of brim. Pin and sew on binding. Place top facing and finish with a wire (Figs. 60 and 61).

Upturning. Place top facing first, then sew upstanding fold. Attach underfacing.

Maline folds. The above instructions apply to maline with some exceptions. As before mentioned, maline is cut lengthwise of the material. It must be cut wide enough to fold several times, four to six and sometimes more. Do not press it with an iron or join seams. Merely overlap material and catch lightly with edges turned under.

SHIRRED EDGES

Use the above methods, but cut strip with allowance for fullness. One and one-half times the circumference is a guide to follow for fullness. Different materials require more or less, according to thickness.

Method No. 1. Gather strip separately on each side, place edge of brim between the two gatherings, and baste. Attach material to upper and lower sides of brim, finishing with wire.

Method No. 2. Gather the two edges and put strip on underside of brim. Fasten facing to shirred strip. The same method may be used to produce varied effects, such as moving this binding to any part of brim, making one piece wide and the other narrow or vice versa. It makes no difference which one is attached. All depends upon the materials and which line is to be emphasized.

Method No. 3. Sew in a wire or cord on each side of fold, then attach fold by placing brim between the two sides. In this case both sides of brim are covered to extend just under shirred edge. Plaitings of any kind may be used in the same manner.

EDGE FINISHES AND BINDING

SECTIONAL FACINGS

A dark hat is made more attractive by the use of contrasting facing on the underside of the brim near the face. The two-color effect in facing of underbrim is called a *sectional facing* (Fig. 62). It may be made of two bias folds or with a continuous flat facing fitted to the brim with no seam. This is often used for georgettes and other thin material. If a contrast in dark and light colors is desired, place light material near face; or, if it is reversed, put on the covering for the underfacing which is light. The size of underfacing depends upon the effect desired. The top facing, which is dark, should be stretched as directed for making hats with edge catch-stitched. The edge of the underfacing may also be dark. Stretch underfacing to brim as for a plain covering. Do not cut out headsize. Finish outer edge with wire. Measure from edge toward headsize any depth of facing desired, cut, allowing $\frac{1}{2}$ inch for turning under.

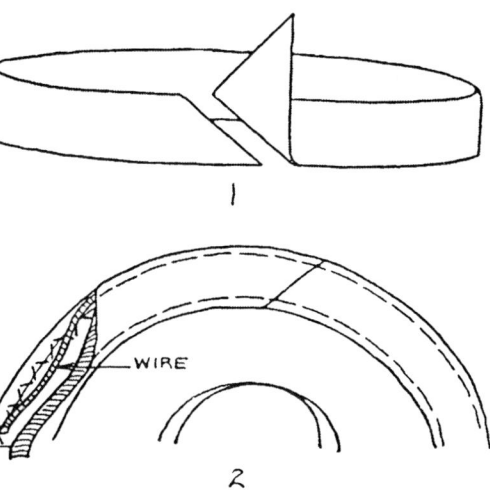

FIG. 62. (*1*) *Joining bias;* (*2*) *sectional facing*

To turn this edge over a wire or finish with a slip stitch, snip edge at intervals of 1 inch not more than $\frac{1}{4}$ inch deep all around.

For bias sectional facing cut, stretch, and join as directed on page 96. Prepare by turning outer edge of material over a wire and finish as in Fig. 62. Inner edge may be finished likewise or with slip stitch.

Crowns as well as brims can be made in sections with the cord finish. Small hats or turbans are effective with such decorations.

CORD FINISHING

Cords are used for edge finishes and for trimmings. For cords to be inserted between two materials see page 110, "Hats Made from Strips of Silk or Ribbon with Cord Edge."

For a *finished* cord to be used on the surface of the hat proceed as follows: For foundation use cable cord, several strands of yarn, or candlewicking. If stiffness is desired in cord, attach tie wire to end of cord and twist at long intervals around cord.

Measure around cord and cut bias strips. Allow $\frac{3}{8}$ to $\frac{1}{2}$ inch for making.

Method No. 1. Measure length of bias strip. Allow twice as much cord plus 2 inches. Beginning at one end of cord, fold bias strip over cord with right side in. Baste, if necessary, and stitch or sew by hand. Do not stitch too near cord or it will not turn easily. Secure end of bias strip to middle of cord by stitching across end. Trim seam if necessary to avoid bulkiness.

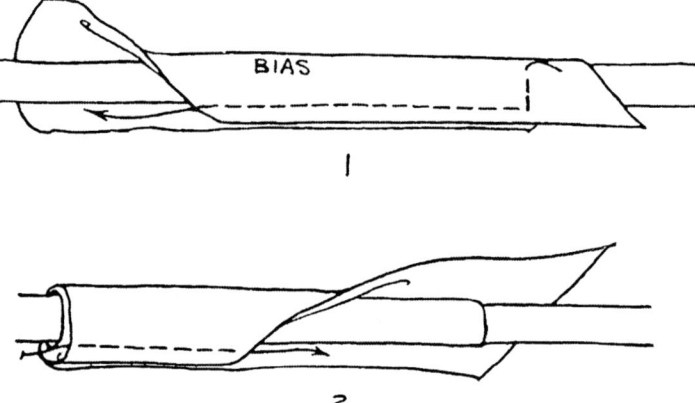

FIG. 63. (*1*) *Covering cord with bias strip;* (*2*) *turning strip over cord*

Begin at stitched end of casing and gradually pull it over uncovered cord as the casing of an umbrella is drawn on. Cut off uncovered cord (Fig. 64, page 105).

EDGE FINISHES AND BINDING

The same method may be used for a soft cord having no foundation. In this case attach a strong double thread inside the length of casing instead of the cable. Draw thread out, pulling

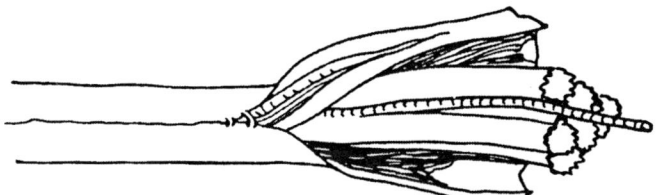

FIG. 64. *Cord made with bias strip over yarn or cord and tie wire*

casing inside out. This form of cord is particularly suitable for pliable stems on flowers, fruits, or berries.

Method No. 2. This may be used for short lengths of cord, but is slower than Method No. 1. Prepare bias strip in the same way. Use cord of equal length. Fold strip over cord and turn edges to wrong side. Hem folded edges together. Place this seam at back of cord.

Splicing cord. Divide stands of cord equally at each end and cut $\frac{1}{2}$ inch from one of these divisions at either end. Overlap ends and sew.

CHAPTER XII

TYPES OF HATS AND THEIR CONSTRUCTION

Making the Sports Hat

Soft Hat of Bias Folds: Headsize—Folds—Lining for Folds—Basting Together—Sewing to Frame—Underside of Brim

Bias Folds with Running Stitch for Decorating

Bias Folds Decorated with Narrow Hemp Braid and Running Stitches

Crown of Bias Folds: Crinoline Foundation—Sewing Folds to Crown—Attaching Crown to Brim

Hats Made from Strips of Silk or Ribbon with Cord Edge: Finishing Edge of Brim—Underfacing—Crown

Crown with a Wire Cord

Underfacing of Radiating Strips with a Cord Edge

Ribbon Hat No. 1: Covering Brim and Crown

Ribbon Hat No. 2: Covering

Ribbon Hat No. 3 (without Frame): Headsize—Crown

Making Brim with Cords: Headsize—Material for Brim—Sewing in Cords—Sewing to Headsize—Crowns

Shirred Hat of Silk: Measuring Sections for Stitching—Stitching Strip—Shaping Frame—Sewing Brim—Finishing Tip

Silk Hat Stitched or Hemstitched: Underfacing—Finishing Edge of Brim—Crown—Headsize

Tucked Brim: Materials—Shaping Brim—Making Crown

Halo Brim No. 1: Materials—Making

Halo Brim No. 2: Materials—Crowns—Making—Headband or Crown

Child's Stitched Hat: Materials—Pattern—Cutting—Basting—Making—Finishing Headsize—Crown—Trimmings

Tam-o'-Shanter: Eight Types

MAKING THE SPORTS HAT

The sports hat is easier for the beginner than a plain covered frame. The sports type is usually soft or has merely a crinoline

HATS AND THEIR CONSTRUCTION

interlining and occasionally a fine wire on the edge. Such a hat requires little or no trimming, because it is decorative in its construction. The color, too, is more varied and daring than in the more conservative and dressy hat.

SOFT HAT OF BIAS FOLDS

Follow previous instructions in pattern cutting and make desired shape for hat brim. Adjust shape to head to be sure of headsize and size of brim. Place pattern on crinoline and cut out, following edge of pattern. Allow for an overlap at seams only when fullness has been taken from edge of brim to give drooping or upturning effect. Allow usual $\frac{3}{4}$ inch at headsize.

Headsize. Wire headsize with usual frame wire. Sew around headsize a $\frac{3}{4}$-inch band made of willow, buckram, or a double piece of crinoline, or any kind of material that is stiff enough to give body to the headsize. A piece of flat ribbon wire $\frac{1}{2}$ inch wide is sometimes put around headsize instead of frame wire. This gives a softer effect. Or, a band may be sewed around headsize without any wires, making a much softer hat.

Folds. Follow previous instructions for measuring and cutting bias strips (twice the width plus making). Join strips and press seam open.

Lining for folds. Cut a bias strip of crinoline or cambric one-half the width of a silk strip.

Basting together. Fold width of silk strips through middle and place crinoline or cambric between the two. Pin and baste them together. Take care to keep silk folded evenly in basting pieces together. Stretch outer or folded edge of bias strip slightly, in order to sew it to crinoline brim without fullness.

Sewing to crinoline frame. Begin on top side at back of brim. Hold brim in hands in order to sew from right to left, allowing brim to hang down in lap, but not to rest there. This method of holding the brim prevents the shape from being distorted. Extend fold about $\frac{1}{4}$ inch from edge of crinoline, pin it in place, and sew the two together about ¼ inch from cut edge of fold. A little fullness will occur at inner edge in sewing fold around hat, but if outer edge is stretched with fingers there will not be much fullness to dispose of inside. When first row has been completed, carry fold on around, gradually sloping it until the two folds overlap one-half the width of the fold or less. Care must be taken to overlap the two folds so the foundation of crinoline will not show. If outer edge is not sewed down, a wider overlap is required. Continue to sew folds around brim until it is covered. If there is any irregularity in outline of hat, some parts of brim will be covered before other parts are finished. In this case, fill the vacant part by sewing short lengths of folds on top of each other until the frame is covered. Take care to start each strip well up on headsize band and see that crown fits brim without any unfinished places in evidence.

Underside of brim. Place bias folds on underside in same manner as top. The two edges must be caught together with a slip stitch near crinoline to hold them in place. Ends of folds should be carried up on headsize band so crown will cover them.

BIAS FOLDS WITH RUNNING STITCH FOR DECORATION

In making this type of hat the method of attaching the folds may vary. Instead of sewing back edge of fold to crinoline, use embroidery floss and attach fold with running stitch about ¼ inch from folded edge. Floss may be the same color as silk or a contrast, making it more of a decoration. It will not be necessary to catch raw edge of fold down, except with pins, as running stitches will hold the two together.

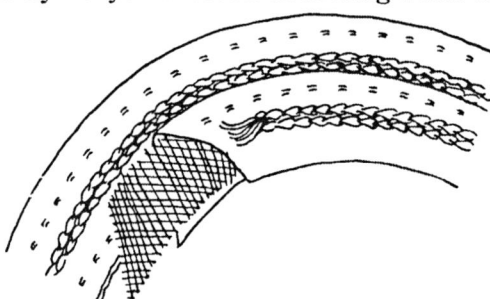

FIG. 65. *Brim made of bias folds decorated with hemp braid and stitches*

HATS AND THEIR CONSTRUCTION

BIAS FOLDS DECORATED WITH NARROW HEMP BRAID AND RUNNING STITCHES

Cut and make folds as directed above. Stretch folded side between fingers, causing folds to curve. Be careful not to stretch the inside. Stitch narrow hemp braid or other decoration near center of fold (Fig. 65). It will not be necessary to sew the two edges together with slip stitches because running stitches will hold them in place. It may be necessary to gather edge of fold.

CROWN OF BIAS FOLDS

In making a crown for either of the above hats prepare folds in same manner as those for brim.

Crinoline foundation. Mold and make crinoline crown as for previous work.

Sewing folds to crown. Begin at center back and at base of crown. Pin fold slightly below base of crown and sew it in either of the above ways to match brim. Overlap first row as for brim and continue to sew around until crown is covered (Fig. 66). When top is covered, cut end, turn it under, and catch it in place. Pin and work very carefully as tip of crown is being covered, because inner or cut edge tends to ripple.

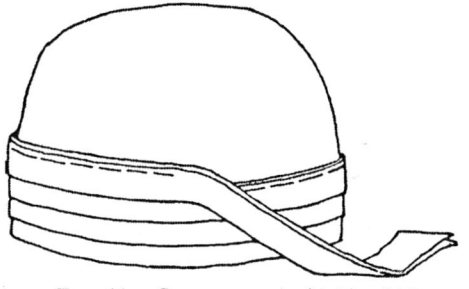

FIG. 66. *Crown covered with bias folds*

It may be necessary as crown nears completion to pin and sew down cut edge of fold before placing last rows. Stretch more, if possible, on outer edge to avoid fullness. Be careful not to misshape crown in stretching the folds on.

Attaching crown to brim. Pin brim and crown together, sew them in place. Finish with any desired trimming. This style of hat as a rule requires little or no trimming.

HATS MADE FROM STRIPS OF SILK OR RIBBON WITH CORD EDGE

Cut several straight strips of silk about $1\frac{3}{4}$ inches wide or use ribbon. Join strips and press them. Fold one side of silk over a cable cord about $\frac{1}{2}$ inch. Baste silk in place and stitch it; or stitch casing first, then run in cord with a bodkin. Gather cut edges. Make same crinoline foundation for this hat as for one of bias folds.

Finishing edge of brim. The edge may be bound with a fold of the same material or with a contrasting color before brim coverings are attached. In binding the edge place cord even with edge or set it back a little. Begin at back, extend cord beyond edge of crinoline, and sew around brim. Use same color of thread that was used for stitching in cord. Place needle in machine stitches, making a long stitch on underside. This will prevent stitches from showing on right side. Draw in gathering thread until fold fits brim. Pin fold in place and gradually slope second row of folds so that they will overlap, as in hat made of bias folds. Continue to sew folds around brim until it is covered.

Underfacing. Any style of facing may be used for the underside. It may be the same as the top if desired, or it may be made of heavy yarns in contrasting colors. Begin at back, just under edge cord, and sew yarn, row after row around until brim is covered, giving a yarn surface. It is tedious to cover the brim in this way because yarn is small and does not fill up quickly, but the unique effect is worth the trouble.

Crown. Follow instructions for making crown of bias folds. Beginning at base, work toward top until crown is finished.

CROWN WITH A WIRE CORD

With a little care, attractive crowns may be made with straight or bias strips. Instead of cord, run a wire in casing. Begin at base near back and pin folds around a mold or block (see "Crown Mold," page 49) until block is covered, including finish at top.

HATS AND THEIR CONSTRUCTION

Remove crown from mold and sew edges together. Be careful to fold wires and bend, shaping them to lines of crown. If a wire crown is convenient (one that has been made for a mold), pin strips around this shape and sew them in place before removing them from frame. Avoid catching stitches around the wire of mold. Strips finished with cable cord in edge or bias strips of velvet or silk may be made in the same manner, giving a soft effect.

UNDERFACING OF RADIATING STRIPS WITH A CORD EDGE

The strips with a cord edge make an interesting underfacing. Divide brim into four parts. Cut strips so that they radiate from headsize to edge of brim plus 1 inch. Gradually fill in each section, overlapping strips at headsize as necessary. Several rows of yarn attached to alternating strips are effective. To make this style of facing, the underside must first be finished so that ends at edge of brim can be turned to top. The top covering will finish the edge.

RIBBON HATS

No. 1. An entirely different effect is obtained by the use of ribbon about 2 inches wide or strips of silk. Instead of folding edge of ribbon to wrong side over cord, fold it to right side, turning over about ¾ inch. Stitch as directed for previous work. The ribbon turned back to the right side makes a little frill and tends to soften the

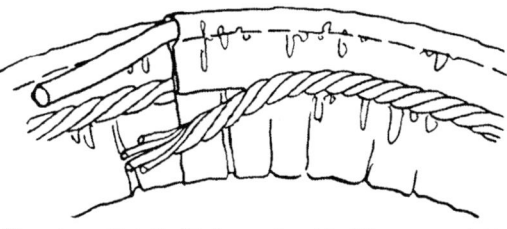

FIG. 67. *Detail of brim made with ribbon or straight strip and decorated with yarn*

hat. The frill turns toward headsize and runs up on crown. Place cord as above. Yarn may be sewed to edge of frill (Fig. 67).

Covering brim and crown. (See "Hats Made from Strips of Silk or Ribbon with Cord Edge," page 110.)

No. 2. The same crinoline foundation may be used if desired; place a small lace wire on the edge to give more body; see "Frame Making" and make a frame that will hold its shape.

Covering. See previous instructions for covering hat with bias folds. The ribbon must be gathered at the inner edge and may be sewed on a little full if desired. In putting on gathered ribbon, first cover frame with same color as ribbon to prevent frame from showing. This covering may be made of cotton crêpe or any other inexpensive material.

No. 3 (without frame). Any shape or untrimmed hat may be used for this style. Preferably choose an upturning brim. Pin ribbon (about 2 inches wide) to underside of frame on the edge. Cut and join the ribbon each time around, overlapping it about $\frac{1}{4}$ inch. Gather inner edge to fit brim. Place remaining rows in same manner, overlapping them $\frac{1}{4}$ inch. Pin and baste them together.

Headsize. Gather ribbon to fit hat at headsize. To hold fullness in place stick in a pin and wind thread around it.

Crown. Pin ribbon to outside of crown, beginning at lower edge. Cut and join each row as for brim. At top, instead of continuing with ribbon, sew two pieces together and cut an oval with seam running from front to back. Place this piece on top of crown under last row of ribbon which is to be gathered and sewed to the oval. Before removing oval piece from crown, carefully mark front, back, and sides. Pin this over the brim, which must be marked in same manner, and baste in place. Stitch each row by machine. Stitch brim twice at each section, the distance of overlap. Stitch on side which is to be the underfacing. Stitch crown from right side also.

MAKING BRIM WITH CORDS

For this style of brim, no interlining is needed to assist in shaping the brim. It is adjusted to suit the individual at each wearing.

Headsize. Make a $\frac{3}{4}$-inch band for headsize if desired.

HATS AND THEIR CONSTRUCTION

Material for brim. Cut material twice the width of brim plus 1 inch for making. The circumference depends upon the number of cords placed in strip. One-half inch is about the average quantity for each cord. Four groups of five cords each in the strip give $2\frac{1}{2}$ inches for each group of five, making a total of 10 inches in all. Measure circumference of brim plus 10 inches for cords and an additional inch for making. Join strip entirely of cords spaced at regular intervals of 1 inch or more around brim.

Sewing in cords. Cable cord of any kind may be used for cording. Two strands of yarns make a soft, effective cord. Fold material over cord and sew it in place by hand or by machine.

Sewing to headsize. Fold strip through the middle, divide in quarters. Divide headsize band in quarters, plait or gather side with cut edges, pin it to headsize band and adjust it to head, then sew. The shape is varied somewhat by pushing fullness to different parts of brim. (See instructions for making frames of flexible nets, page 47.)

Crowns. Make any style desired from foregoing instructions.

SHIRRED HAT OF SILK

In making this style of hat (Fig. 68), the crown and brim are constructed in one piece. To approximate the quantity of material, measure a hat that is about the desired size. It may be changed to a larger or smaller size in the following manner:

Place tape measure at center of crown tip, then pass it straight over crown, down to base of crown, following lines of hat to edge of brim. Multiply this dimension by two and add $1\frac{1}{2}$ inches for making. Measure edge of brim for circumference of hat and to this add 2 inches for overlap. No definite rule can be given, because it depends upon the effect desired. The circumference plus $\frac{1}{8}$ yard may be added, or one and one-half times the circumference, depending upon fullness desired. Take, for example, a medium-sized hat measuring from crown tip to edge of brim $10\frac{1}{2}$ inches. Add $1\frac{1}{2}$ inches. Multiply by two, giving 24 inches for the hat. The circumference of the hat measures 40 inches plain. Add 5 inches, making a total of 45 inches or $1\frac{1}{4}$ yards. Cut a strip 24 inches wide and 45 inches long. Fold it through the middle, making the piece measure 12 inches in width. Pin the two pieces together.

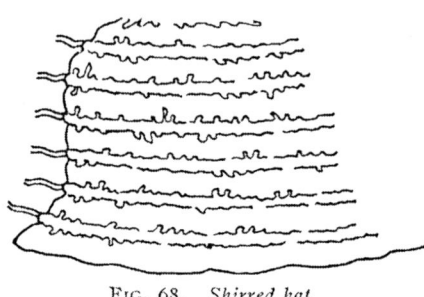

FIG. 68. *Shirred hat*

Measuring sections for stitching. Place this strip on the table and measure from fold 1 inch or less. Draw a line parallel with edge of fold. Measure from this line $\frac{1}{2}$ inch and draw a line. Continue alternating 1-inch and $\frac{1}{2}$-inch spacings until strip contains five or six $\frac{1}{2}$-inch sections.

Stitching strip. Stitch $\frac{1}{2}$-inch markings with silk of same or a contrasting color, or have strip hemstitched. Run $\frac{1}{4}$-inch ribbon wire, the circumference of brim, into the $\frac{1}{2}$-inch casing.

Shaping frame. Draw up material on wire, deciding first the line for headsize. Place shirrings on a crown mold and draw up material, using mold as a guide. Pin strips together. Then draw up brim strips while material is still on crown mold. Shape brim by making it straight, rolling, or drooping. Remove frame from block and get effect by trying it on head. If no corrections are needed, join frame at center back with overlap seam (Fig. 68).

Sewing brim. Make a lapped seam by turning top piece under to wrong side about $\frac{1}{4}$ inch and turn up underpiece to right side, placing one piece directly over the other, and slip-stitch both sides in place.

Finishing tip. Gather fullness in closely at tip. Place edges together. Make a seam about 2 inches long from front to back, sew, and press it with fingers. A button is sometimes placed on top of tip for a finish; or a small patch of same material is put under shirrings sewed to plain piece.

HATS AND THEIR CONSTRUCTION

SILK HAT STITCHED OR HEMSTITCHED

Cut pattern as for previous work. Pin pattern to silk and cut material ½-inch larger on edge. Chalk and baste edge line. Do not slash headsize. Cut ¾ inch in from headsize. If the brim requires a seam, sew and press it. Divide brim into four parts—front, back, and sides, marking it with pins.

Cut flat ribbon wire ¼ inch wide and baste it to brim in a design. The pieces may radiate from headsize to edge of brim. Turn wire down flat at edge and stop within ¼ inch of finished edge (Fig. 69).

To make a more interesting line, proceed as follows: Measure from headsize to edge, bend wire at right angles, then, 3 inches from this line, bend wire again at right angles, and continue length to headsize. This makes a rectangular outline on brim. Pin and baste wire in place and continue with every pair of radiating lines. Put in eight or twelve wires. The number of pairs depends upon the style of the hat. There must be a space between each pair in order to stitch by machine or hemstitch. The wires at headsize must conform to shape radiating from edge.

Underfacing. Cut and baste underfacing carefully in place. Baste around each wire so bastings can be used as a guide for stitching. Sew or hemstitch around each piece on inside. Stitch division line between each pair of wires from edge to headsize, then finish edge.

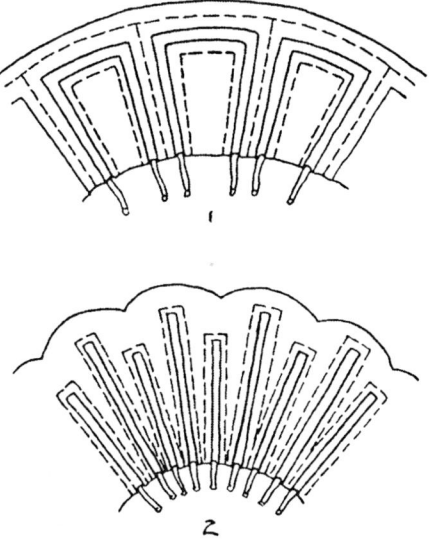

FIG. 69. (1) *Stitched or hemstitched brim braced with ribbon wire*; (2) *variation in method of placing wire*

Finishing edge of brim. The edge of brim may be picoted or bound with a fold, or buttonholed or blanket-stitched with yarn.

Crown. Cut crown in two pieces—top and side band; or use the sectional crown. If the former is used, baste top and side band together, stitch or hemstitch. The side band may be left plain or draped slightly. The sectional crown may be stitched, hemstitched, or finished with cord.

Headsize. Cut a narrow band of stiff material, or use ribbon wire $\frac{1}{2}$ inch wide and make the size of head. Pin material over frame, slash brim at headsize, and sew it in place. Attach it to crown. This type of hat may be made of velvet, duvetyn, or any other fabric suitable for soft sports hats.

TUCKED BRIM

Materials. Silk, ribbon, or maline may be used for this type of brim. Maline must be folded at least four times for sufficient weight.

Cut a strip of material the circumference of the brim desired, either bias or straight, and twice the width plus $1\frac{1}{2}$ inches for finishing at headsize. Join ends of strip by machine and press. (Do not press maline with an iron.) Fold width of strip through middle and pin it in place. Cut and straighten several pieces of frame wire, about $1\frac{1}{2}$ inches shorter than width of strip when folded through middle. Sew wires in material by folding material over wire, forming little tucks through both or all thicknesses. Begin to work from cut edge. Wires must not extend the width of the strip, but must be from 1 to 2 inches shorter so the outer edge will droop or roll up, giving a ruffled effect. Place wires about $1\frac{1}{2}$ inches apart around the strip, being careful to catch each one once or twice so that it will not pull out.

Make a headband $\frac{3}{4}$ inch wide, wired on one edge. Cover lower edge with a bias fold of material. Divide the tucked strip into halves, quarters, and eighths. Pin to headband and sew strip in place. Plait or gather fullness and fasten wires securely.

Shaping brim. Bend wires gradually in place to suit the individual.

Making crown. Any type may be used. See chapters ii and v.

HALO BRIM NO. 1

A type of hat known as the *halo* has a single edge wire with no spokes, having material stretched tightly from edge to head-size. This hat was first made of transparent material and gave a halo effect. It is successful only in case of perfect workmanship.

Materials. Silk or ribbon is most suitable for this hat. Organdy or maline may be used.

Making. Measure and cut steel wire the circumference of finished brim. Join wire with a clip. Cut a straight piece of material for hat the circumference of wire plus seam, and twice width of brim plus 2 inches for a fold on the edge and $1\frac{1}{2}$ inches for attaching to headband or crown. Join ends of strip by machine and press. Fold strip in half through middle. Stitch about 1 inch in from fold the length of strip of material and pin the wire in place close to stitching line. Divide inner or cut edges of strip in halves and quarters and plait to headband or crown.

Take care in attaching brim and headband. Draw the material in snugly to make the brim firm.

This type of brim may be made of one strip of ribbon the width of brim by folding edge over so as to make extension and casing for wire. Or two contrasting colors of ribbon may be used. Stitch edges together, then stitch the two pieces together near edge. If desired, after steel wire is placed between the two pieces, a second stitching may be made, forming a casing for the wire.

HALO BRIM NO. 2

Materials. Any kind of soft material may be used for this hat—organdy, georgette, maline, gingham, etc. The brim is not to be shaped, i. e., drooping or upturning, but must be some form of sailor or other straight brim. When making a hat of organdy use two thicknesses for the brim; of georgette, four or more thicknesses; of maline, use more than of georgette.

Crowns. Any type of soft or stiff crown may be used. This depends upon prevailing styles.

Making. Measure and cut steel wire as above directed. Place material flat on table and put a circle of wire on the material. Pin it in place. Mark halves, quarters, and eighths. Continue to pin until material is tight and smooth. Cut material about $\frac{3}{8}$ inch larger than wire. Turn material over the wire. With stab stitch sew it in place near wire.

The edge may be finished with bias folds any width, or with a narrow binding of the same or contrasting materials, as braid or ribbon.

Headband or crown. Place headband at any part of the halo to obtain desired shape. It may be in the center, nearer the back than the front, or more to one side. Pin it in place. Cut the material about $1\frac{1}{2}$ inches inside headline. Slash at one-inch intervals. Pin it in place. Try hat on to see that the slashed pieces are drawn in tightly enough to adjust the brim securely. Sew them in place.

CHILD'S STITCHED HAT

Materials. Any suitable wash fabric such as gingham, chambray, or linen; taffeta; or any lightweight woolen goods, as broadcloth, venetian, or novelty suiting, may be used. The interlining may be Indianhead, lightweight duck, linen-canvas, or crash.

Pattern. Measure a hat to find desired size for brim. This will be determined by size of child's head and shape of face. Suppose headsize is 19 inches and brim is to be 12 inches in diameter. (See "Cutting Brim," page 13.) Cut another paper circle from a 7-inch square. Refold in quarters. From cut edge measure down on double fold $\frac{3}{4}$ inch. From single fold measure on cut edge 1 inch. Connect the two points with a gradual

HATS AND THEIR CONSTRUCTION

curve, thus forming an oval which is the shape the headsize should be. Place the oval on the large circle of paper, either in the center for an even brim, or 1 inch or more from the center for a poke-bonnet effect. The latter will give greater protection from the sun. This will make a flat circular hat with no seam. To remove flare from brim and make it droop, place a tiny plait at edge of brim in center, gradually sloping it to headsize. Be careful not to diminish headsize. Take similar plait in back and on each side. To increase the droop, add plaits halfway between these. Cut brim open at center back.

Cutting. It is advisable to shrink interlining and other wash fabrics before cutting them. Fold material and cut two thicknesses of interlining. Place pattern on cloth with center-front line lengthwise. Cut outer edge according to pattern. Leave $\frac{1}{4}$-inch seam at back and around headsize. From this pattern cut two pieces of material for the outside, allowing $\frac{1}{4}$ inch for seams.

Basting. Place each piece of interlining on wrong side of cloth (both upper and lower) so that edges are together at headsize and the cloth extends $\frac{1}{4}$ inch beyond the lining at the outside. To baste, place lining on table and lay the cloth over it, smoothing and stretching. Join two pieces with irregular basting. Baste several times around the brim.

Making. Place right sides of brims together. Baste and stitch around outside, just catching edge of interlining. Open back seams and join the two pieces with $\frac{1}{4}$-inch seam. Turn brim inside out. Crease edge back to stitching as in a French seam. Baste carefully along edge and stitch as desired with evenly spaced rows covering brim, or with fancy patterns, as zigzag or scroll.

Finishing headsize. After stitching try brim on the child's head. Cut a straight piece of cloth 2 inches wide and the length of headsize plus $1\frac{1}{2}$ inches for making. Measure this to headsize to see that they are equal. Baste and stitch this strip to headsize in ¼-inch seam. Slash headsize at 1-inch intervals as far as stitching. Turn other side of strip over stitching as in a skirt band, and stitch. This forms a support for the crown. Remove bastings and press brim.

Crown. The crown may be a plain circle, bound or otherwise finished on the edge and buttoned to headsize band; or made larger and gathered with a ruffle and attached. It may be a gathered circle attached to a band and basted to the hat after washing; or the band may be buttoned to the headsize strip.

Trimmings. A chambray hat may be attractively finished with white rickrack stitched to the edge of brim and crown. A white hat may be made more dressy by the use of a simple lace edge, slightly gathered, or a tiny ruffle of embroidery. A taffeta hat (this may be made from an old dress) may have narrow plaiting set between edges of brim before brim is stitched. Instead, a narrow double plaiting of ribbon or silk, picoted on both edges, may be used. It is preferable to use moderately stiff linen-canvas interlining for the silk or wool hat. Either of these may be finished around the edge with a binding of ribbon attached with a running stitch or French knots. The silk hat may be further ornamented with silk or ribbon bows, handmade silk flowers, wool crocheted flowers, or rosettes of plaiting. See "Handmade Trimmings," pages 123 ff.

TAM-O'-SHANTER

The tam-o'-shanter (see "The Story of the Hat," chapter xviii) is a type of headgear which is worn ordinarily by small children and schoolgirls. It is sometimes in vogue for older women. The tam crown on a hat is a modification of the cap.

A variety of materials may be employed in making the tam—wash goods (usually white), flannel, serge, broadcloth, velvet, or other dress goods. It may be made to match the suit or coat. The material need not be new.

HATS AND THEIR CONSTRUCTION

The making is simple. It consists of stitching to give a tailored effect. A ribbon band with ends or tabs at the side may be added for a finish.

In order to determine size of top, cut a piece of paper or cloth and try it on. The dimensions given below represent an average size.

The following directions for cutting show various modifications of tams.

No. 1. Cut two circles 13 inches in diameter. Cut headsize from one circle (see page 13, "Cutting Headsize"). Take head measurement and cut band this length plus seams, and 3 inches wide. Fold band lengthwise through middle and attach to headsize in the circle. This makes a finished band about 1 inch wide. Join the two circles in a seam. The seam may be finished with a cord. Wool materials may have a lining both in the tam and in the band.

No. 2. Cut circle 13 inches in diameter for tip. Cut band 4 inches wide and length of circumference of circle plus seams. Attach this to the circle in a seam.

Painting by Rembrandt
Fig. 70. *Tam*

Gather lower edge of band and attach it to a headband as for No. 1.

No. 3. Cut two 13-inch squares. From one square cut headsize, finish with band, and sew together as for No. 1. This tam, instead of being round, has four corners.

No. 4. This is similar to No. 2 except that a 9-inch square is used instead of the circle. Make as for No. 2, using the 4-inch band gathered to the narrow band.

No. 5. This is the so-called artist's tam (Fig. 70). Cut a circle 16 inches in diameter. Gather edge and attach it to narrow band as for No. 1.

No. 6. This makes a square, flat tam with four sections on top. Cut a 17-inch square. Fold corners to center on wrong side where they meet. Join in seams, either plain or with cord. Cut headsize from plain side of square and finish with band as for No. 1.

No. 7. This is a round tam having a circular side band attached to the band with or without gathers. (See page 22, "Curved Side Band.") The pattern may be spread more if desired. Cut circle 13 inches in diameter. Sew it to outer edge of circular side band. Finish with a band as for No. 1.

No. 8. This is a tam made in sections similar to the sectional crown, only larger. (See page 24, "Sectional Crown.") Use a circle 16 inches in diameter. In shaping sections allow for fullness desired. Attach circle to band as for No. 1.

PART V. TRIMMING THE HAT

CHAPTER XIII

HANDMADE TRIMMINGS

Bows: Wiring—Tailored Bow—Tied or Cravat Bow—Alsatian Bows, No. 1 and No. 2—Aigrette Bow—Butterfly Bow

Rosette

Ribbon Cockade with Variations: Cockades Nos. 1-4—Band Trimming of Folded Points: No. 1 and No. 2, Bands; No. 3, Rosette Ball; No. 4, Ribbon or Braid Ornament; No. 5, Pendant

Cord Trimmings

Novelty Trimmings: No. 1, Large Flower in Center—No. 2, Leaves—No. 3, Stem of Leaf—No. 4, Pumpkin or Melon Seed—No. 5, Peanut—No. 6, Ball of Yarn—No. 7, Yarn Twist—No. 8, Chenille Ornament—No. 9, Sealing-Wax Leaf—No. 10, Yarn Ornament—No. 11, Yarn Ornament—No. 12, Yarn Ornament—No. 13, Yarn Ornament

Flowers and Fruit: Velvet Flower—Silk Flower—Futurist Rose: Leaves—Poppy: Making Petal; Making Center; Sewing Petals—Buttonmold Flower: Band Upturned or Collar on Edge—Daisy—Tailored Rose: Materials; Making—Grapes: Materials; Making; Leaves—Organdy Flowers: Putting Center and Organdy Together; Leaves; Making Leaf; Bud; Tendril; Wrapping Stems—To Make Other Types of Organdy Flowers—Yarn Flower No. 1—Yarn Flower No. 2—Crocheted Flower: Making; Stem; Leaf—Straw Flowers and Leaves—Made Quill—Ribbon Plaiting

BOWS

As the painter takes canvas, brush, and paint and creates a picture, so the true designer with ribbon, wire, and needle fashions a bow. Only the artist can originate. The spark of genius is found, however, in many who are not professionals.

Any one may study and copy masterpieces, which in millinery are the best pattern hats. With practice it is possible to acquire appreciation of good bows and some skill in making them. The exceptional person has a gift in the delicate manipulation of materials. In most cases skill is attained only after frequent repetition.

In copying a bow it is not wise for the beginner to work with materials intended for the hat. Rather, make use of old ribbon or strips of cambric or tissue paper.

A bow shows at once whether it was made and fastened to the hat by an experienced trimmer or by an amateur; this difference, however, is apparent only to the trained observer. A fine discrimination between what is good and what is mediocre precedes ability to make a good bow.

Wiring bows. Use flat ribbon wire, frame wire, or lace wire (the last for thin materials, such as lace). Attach wire by sewing or with glue. The edge of ribbon or silk may be stitched to form a casing and the wire run in. The wire may be tacked to the ribbon at intervals. Ribbon or silk may be pasted to flat ribbon wire, or the wire may be pasted between pieces of ribbon.

Tailored bow. The most common use for the tailored bow is on a hatband for a sailor or other tailored hat. The length depends upon the width of the ribbon and the size and height of the crown.

To make a formal band, place ribbon about crown and cut it to fit. Fasten it to crown. Decide upon length of bow. It may have two to four loops, or two loops and two ends, or four cut ends. The waist of the bow or the middle piece may be flat, or plaited, or crushed. It is commonly put on plain.

If ribbon has a right and a wrong side, make all the loops on one side at a time to avoid cutting.

Decide on length of end, which may be cut straight or bias (with long point at base of crown). Fold flat loop a little shorter than end. On opposite side make loop, first coming back to center, and finish with the end. Pin and tack loop.

Place the center piece, tack it on wrong side near tip, bring it down, and tack it at bottom. If there is enough ribbon, the ends may meet or overlap at the center in the back. Tack bow

HANDMADE TRIMMINGS

in place. The small tailored bow is often used to cover the place where trimmings are fastened. The semitailored bow is made practically like the tailored bow. It is less formal and softer. It may be wider and crushed in the center (Fig. 78, page 133, No. 6).

Tied or cravat bow. This is made with two loops and two ends. It is the simplest form of bow and is tied from one piece of ribbon (Fig. 71, No. 3).

Begin with the end of ribbon hanging downward with wrong side of ribbon held toward worker (length of end is determined by size of bow desired). Plait ribbon between thumb and fingers and not in palm of hand. Determine length of loop by trying it against the hat, and bring ribbon toward worker so that wrong side is inside the loop. Place inner selvage between thumb and finger of left hand, meeting the portion formerly plaited. Plait with right hand and place plaited portions together. The plaited portion of the ribbon is spoken of as the *waist* of the bow.

After first loop is made, slip fingers of right hand into loop with a jerky movement to arrange plaitings. Never take hold of ribbon in a way that will flatten end of loop. For next loop turn ribbon from worker, catching edge of selvage between fingers of left hand beside waist of first loop. Plait width of ribbon and place it beside waist of first loop. Do not place plaited portions over one another, as this gives a stiff effect. Slip fingers of left hand under second loop and jerk it slightly to strengthen plaitings. The bow is now ready to be tied.

Still hold it in left hand, with one end and loop extending toward the right and one loop and long end of ribbon extending toward the left. Bring long end of ribbon forward and around waist of bow and pass end through the small loop just formed. This will place one end of bow under one loop and one end of bow over the other loop. Pull long end of ribbon slightly snug, being careful not to have waist of bow too small for proportions of entire bow.

126 HATS AND HOW TO MAKE THEM

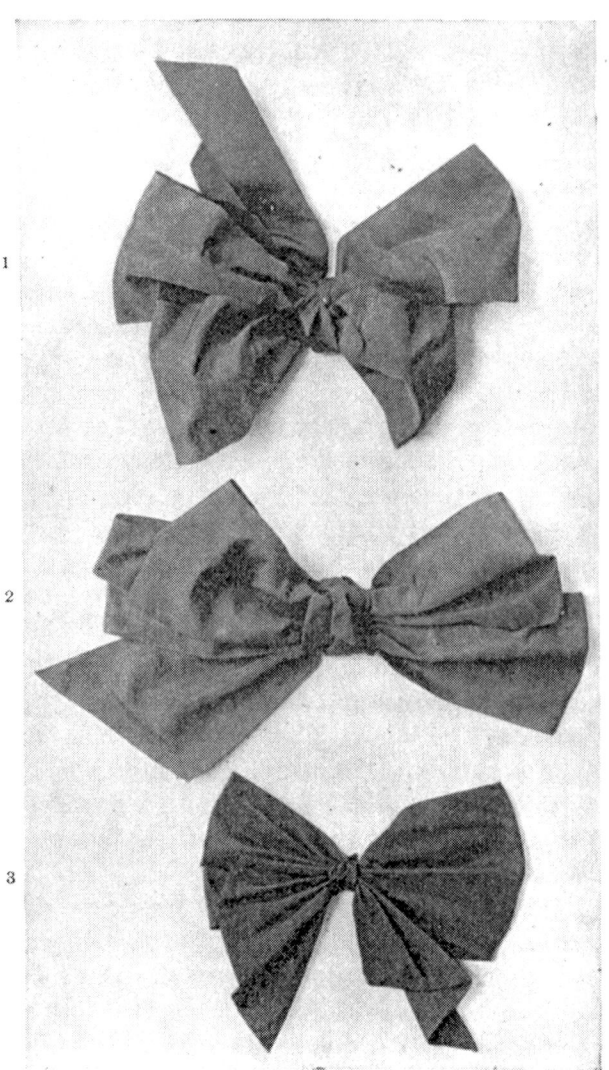

FIG. 71. *Ribbon bows—Alsatian bows*
    1. Over ribbon wire
    2. Over frame wire
    3. Tied or cravat bow

This bow may be varied by making two or more loops on a side, all equal in length or of different lengths.

The uneven bow is like the cravat bow, only the loops are of unequal length and often the waist is not in exact center. It is made like cravat bow. It may be used for a hat.

Alsatian bow. The Alastian bow is made like the cravat bow. The name is derived from the Alsatian headdress. It is sometimes used on nurses' bonnets and on mourning hats. Usually it has two ends and an even number of loops on each side.

HANDMADE TRIMMINGS

Some beginners might find it easier to use tie wire to hold each plaited loop as they go along, but practice makes wiring in simple bows unnecessary.

In making fancy Alsatian bows having several loops or ends, tie wire or needle and thread are necessary to hold the waist of the bow.

If ribbon is long enough do not cut, but finish as for single Alsatian bow. A good effect is obtained by making a plain knot in long end of ribbon near waist or center of bow and then passing long end toward front and around waist and under the plain knot. Cut protruding ends bias, or notch or round them as fashion dictates.

No. 1. Alsatian bow No. 1 (Fig. 71, No. 1) requires 2 yards of ribbon $5\frac{1}{4}$ inches wide. Hold the ribbon over flat ribbon wire as it is being made. Tie-tack in place.

No. 2. Alsatian bow No. 2. Allow 3 inches at waist of bow. To make frame (Fig. 72), measure length of loop, bend wire at right angles, bend again about 2 inches less than the width of the ribbon. Bend a third time, returning to center. Make "frame" for loops. Extend wire to opposite side, bending in same manner. Return to the other side and make a third loop.

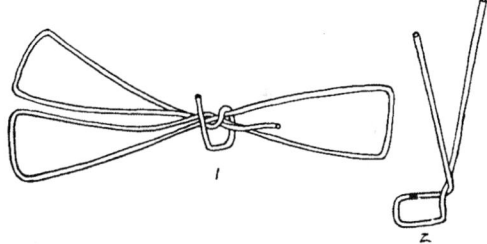

FIG. 72. (*1*) *Frame for Alsation bow;* (*2*) *frame for ends of butterfly bow*

At center, twist end of wire once or twice around the three loops. Cut. Take the 3-inch end and form a smaller loop to be used for attaching to hat. Begin with end of ribbon and fold over loops of frame according to Fig. 71, No. 2. Tack loops to frame from inside.

Aigrette bow (Fig. 73, page 129). No. 1 requires $1\frac{7}{8}$ yards of ribbon $5\frac{1}{4}$ inches wide. Use frame wire as for No. 2 above.

This bow is like the Alsatian bow except for the length of the loops. There are two short ones and two long ones with an end. Fasten with tie wire or needle and thread and insert wire supports afterward. For end of ribbon use a piece of wire 3 inches longer than the upstanding end. Bend loop of wire to be placed at waist of bow (Fig. 72, No. 2). Slip wire up through waist of bow on longer point of cut ribbon to within 1 inch of end. Cover wire by folding ribbon over $\frac{1}{2}$ to $\frac{3}{4}$ inch. Tie-tack ribbon in place. Prepare wire frame for longer loop similar to Alsatian frame and tack. Fasten wire to back of loop from inside. Finish at waist with small loop for attaching. Leave second loop soft and tack it to wired loop from inside. Do not wire short loops.

Tie a soft knot in ribbon and slip the end through it as in illustration on page 129, No. 1.

Butterfly bow. The butterfly bow requires $1\frac{1}{2}$ yards of ribbon $5\frac{1}{4}$ inches wide. Make the bow the same as Alsatian bow with the exception of ends, which should be longer than the four loops. Wire the long sides of cut ends as for the aigrette bow. Do not fail to finish wire with loop at waist for attaching.

ROSETTE

The simplest way to make a rosette is to tie a knot around a series of loops (about the same length). Draw the knot very tightly around waist of bow. Or wind the waist with wire before making the knot. In some materials it is easier to sew the loops in place and the knot afterward. Adjust loops after knot is tied (Fig. 73, No. 4). This may assume the shape of a flat rosette pompon or half-sphere.

A rosette may be made on a wired buckram foundation which can be bent in any form desired. To make, begin at outer edge with loops and sew them in place, working toward center. Any material may be used for loops.

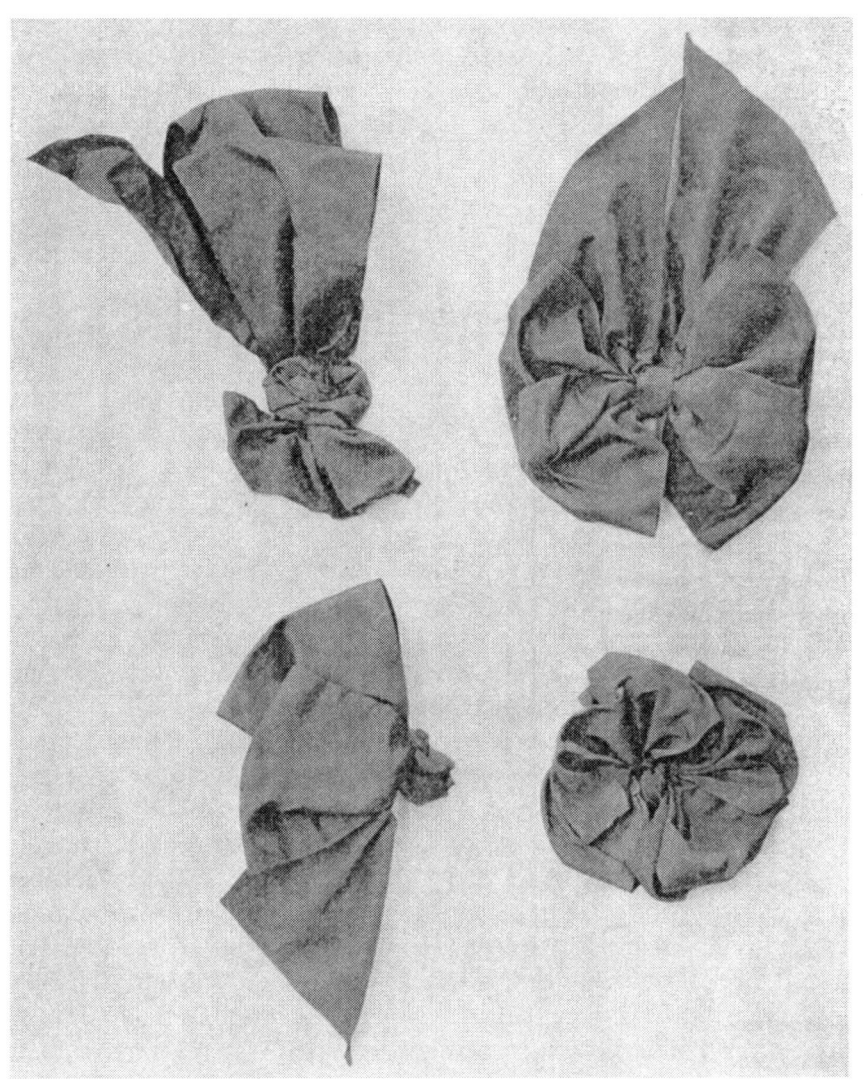

FIG. 73. *Ribbon bows*

1. Upper left—aigrette
2. Lower left—tied or cravat bow with variation
3. Upper right—butterfly
4. Lower right—rosette

A similar effect may be obtained by use of plaitings or shirrings of silk, ribbon, or lace (Fig. 74). The center may be finished with a cabochon, hatpin, ball of fur, bunch of stamens, or group of knots.

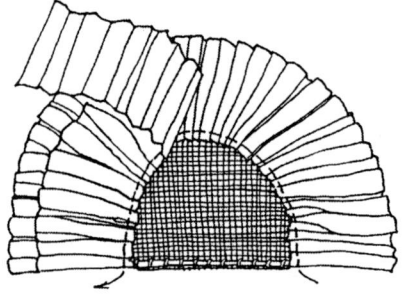

FIG. 74. *Plaitings on wired foundation*

RIBBON COCKADE WITH VARIATIONS

The cockade is a formal rosette made of ribbon, silk, or leather. It originated in France and was worn on a hat as a badge of office or of a political party. It later became a part of livery. The cockade in its many variations (Fig. 75, page 131) is used as trimming on women's semitailored hats. Grosgrain ribbon, because of its stiffness, is usually employed in making the cockade.

The quantity of ribbon required depends upon the width of the ribbon and upon the size and shape of the cockade. Fig. 75, No. 1, requires $1\frac{1}{4}$ yards of ribbon $1\frac{1}{2}$ inches wide (No. 9). For a smaller cockade use narrower ribbon, the length being proportionately less.

Hold ribbon in horizontal position in right hand and with left hand fold cut edge over to lower selvage, forming a triangle. Hold triangle in left hand and with right hand fold top selvage toward the worker until selvages meet, forming two similar triangles. During the folding continue to hold ribbon in left hand. Fold right-hand triangle over to the left-hand triangle. Fold left-hand selvage toward worker, forming a triangle and spreading $\frac{1}{8}$ inch between selvages at base. Fold lower triangle on upper triangle. Fold upper selvage toward worker, spreading $\frac{1}{8}$ inch at base. Fold right-hand triangle over to left. Tack lower points together with invisible stitches. Continue to make triangles until the cockade is of the desired size.

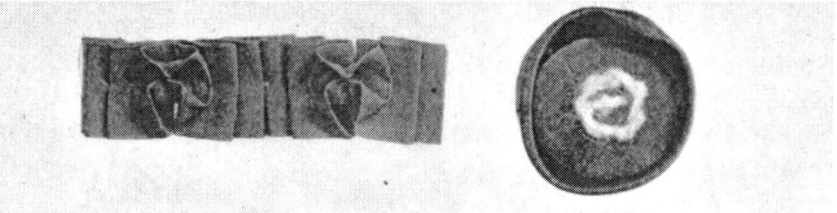

FIG. 75. *Ribbon cockades, plaiting, and buttonmold ornament*

Cockade No. 1. No. 1 on page 131 has thirteen triangles. The points tacked together become the center of the rosette.

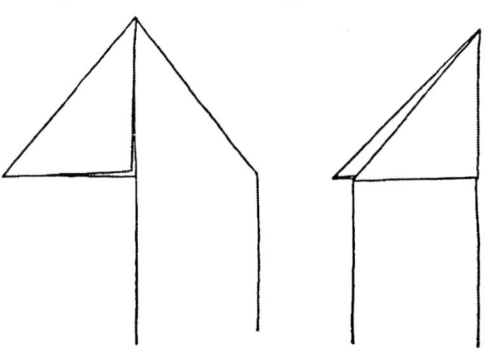

Method 1   Method 2
FIG. 76. *Methods 1 and 2 for making cockade*

In adjusting the rosette to the hat, each point on the outer edge must be tacked in place.

Cockade No. 2. Fold ten triangles or points. Tack points in center as for No. 1. Tack outer points in groups of two. Midway between inner and outer points tack at five places (Fig. 75, No. 2).

Cockade No. 3. Make as many points as desired (twenty-two are shown in illustration), but instead of spreading triangles $\frac{1}{8}$ inch at base spread them $\frac{1}{4}$ inch. Tack points in center as for No. 1 and No. 2. Reverse the rosette, press flat with hand, and tack in place according to Fig. 75, No. 3.

Cockade No. 4. Make twenty-two triangles or points as for No. 3. Fasten center and press flat without reversing and tack each point in place (Fig. 75, No. 4).

Band trimming of folded points (Fig. 78). Use narrow ribbon or braid $\frac{1}{2}$ to 1 inch wide. Prepare as for cockade. Fold triangles, spreading them $\frac{1}{4}$ inch. With needle and thread catch middle of each triangle on long side, which will be the back or base of trimming. Continue to fold and sew triangles until band is desired length.

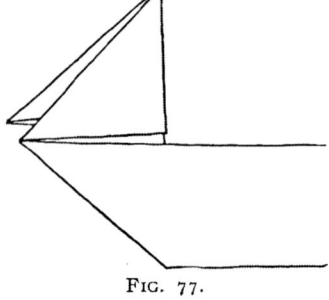

FIG. 77.
Method 3 for making cockade

No. 1 and No. 2, bands. These are made in the same manner, except that No. 1 is allowed to stand up in the center and No. 2 is pressed flat with the fingers. No. 1 is adapted for trimming the base of the crown and No. 2 for the brim.

FIG. 78. *Variations of ribbon cockade and tailored bow*

No. 3, rosette ball. A small ball-like rosette is similar to No. 1 on page 131. Prepare as for large cockade. Tack points in center at both ends and press them flat with fingers.

No. 4, ribbon or braid ornament. This trimming is merely a piece of ribbon or braid folded lengthwise in the middle and coiled. Insert needle in end of material and wind around it to desired size. Sew in place and remove needle.

No. 5, pendant. A ball for a decorative hatpin or an ornament on hat or dress. May be made from narrow ribbon or braid. Proceed as for cockade No. 1. For $\frac{3}{4}$- or 1-inch ribbon make sixteen points. Bring long side of triangles to center and tack all outer points or sharp angles together at both ends (Fig. 78, No. 5).

No. 6, tailored bow. See page 124.

CORD TRIMMINGS

See page 104.

NOVELTY TRIMMINGS

It is possible with patience, skill, and ingenuity to evolve many interesting forms of trimmings for hats. (See Fig. 80, facing this page, for decorations made of yarn, chenille, sealing wax, peanuts, pumpkin or melon seed, buckram, mending tissue, and tie wire.)

No. 1, large flower in center. Cut a piece of paper about $1\frac{5}{8}$ by $1\frac{3}{8}$ inches. Fold it lengthwise through middle. Round the corner, taking more from one end than from the other, making pear-shaped piece. Cut an opening in center, beginning about $\frac{3}{8}$ inch down from edge on folded side, and slope gradually to opposite end. This makes a pattern for the foundation for six buckram petals (Fig. 79). Wind each petal with a fine embroidery yarn, covering buckram. Overlap ends, causing each petal to cup. Sew three of the petals together, forming a shape similar to

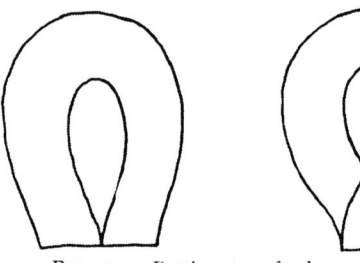

FIG. 79. *Petal pattern for large flower*

FIG. 80. *Novelty trimmings*

For usual decoration made from yarn, chenille, melon seeds, peanuts, and sealing wax. Variety of color and texture has been obtained by combining these materials and applying oil paints for special accents of color. Sheared yarn pompons and knotted effect in chenille and yarn introduce new textures.

See directions for making in text, pages 134–138.

1. Large flower in center
2. Leaves
3. Stem of leaf
4. Pumpkin or melon seed
5. Peanut
6. Ball of yarn
7. Yarn twist
8. Chenille ornaments
9. Sealing wax
10-13. Yarn ornaments

a clover leaf. Place the three remaining petals on top alternating with the others. For this flower use fine white or cream embroidery yarn. Tint each petal pale yellow. Paint over the yellow on the ends of petal a darker color (more of a brown), giving the effect of shading. Tube paints mixed in gasoline or dyes may be used to obtain this effect. Pale yellow yarn may be used. This would require but one color of paint (the darker). In painting the flower it is better to paint each leaf before sewing them together. Notice that some of the petals cup toward the hat and others cup in the opposite direction. Make center of gray-blue sealing wax, molded into a cone shape. On one side of cone put a little dash of vermilion. To attach it to center, heat it slightly and stick it in place.

No. 2, leaves. On each side of flower place two leaves made as follows: Cut buckram foundation $1\frac{1}{2}$ inches long by $\frac{1}{2}$ inch wide; shape it to a point on each end as illustrated. With light green yarn take a few stitches over each end. Then *wind* leaf with yarn to cover it completely. Tack each end with the same color of yarn to hold it in place.

No. 3, stem of leaf. Cover a piece of tie wire with brown silk floss by winding floss around wire. Fasten ends securely. Place brown-covered wire over center of leaf and catch it in place with stitches crossing the brown wire; or take two stitches near together extending slightly toward edge, giving the irregular effect of the natural leaf.

No. 4, pumpkin or melon seed. Use seven seeds for this ornament. Tint each seed slightly, making center or small end of the seed darker. (Color used in illustration is a very dark blue-green.) Pierce a hole about $\frac{3}{16}$ or $\frac{1}{4}$ inch from small end of each seed. If seed is too brittle, soak it in water. Take about 8 or 10 inches of uncovered tie wire and run it through hole in seed. Pull wire halfway through, then make four or five tight twists. The wire extending from the small end makes a stem to hold the seed in place. Finish each seed in this manner. Group the seven together, being careful to keep dark sides turned toward center. Wind an extra piece of uncovered tie wire just below (about $\frac{1}{4}$ inch) ends of seeds to hold them in place. Bend each seed back, forming flowerlike petals. Wind stem with mending tissue cut in $\frac{1}{2}$-inch strips.

No. 5, peanut. Prepare four peanuts in the following manner: Dye two or stain them a dark plum or violet color. Leave the others natural color and cover all four with clear shellac or lacquer. On end of the light peanuts put a touch of darker color. Pierce a hole near one end of peanut and run covered tie wire through it, then twist the ends as for finishing the pumpkin seed. Cover the half-inch of peanut nearest the stem with milliner's glue and wind it with dark green chenille. Attach a light and a dark peanut to stem of pumpkin seed. Begin to wind stem where wire joins peanut, keeping chenille in regular lines and close together, until six or seven strands are put on. Then bring end of chenille back to starting place (at the end of peanut) and wind it around wire, covering stem. Each stem should be about 6 inches long finished. Cover another piece of wire 3 or 4 inches long with chenille. Curve one end and place it just under the pumpkin seed. Join the four pieces together with uncovered tie wire and cover the joining with mending tissue or chenille.

No. 6, ball of yarn. At base of crown at center front under seed petals make an ornament of henna yarn. For this size, measuring $1\frac{1}{2}$ inches in diameter, take about 15 yards of knitting yarn. Spread the two fingers slightly, and wind the yarn around them. Twist tie wire or heavy thread tightly around center of yarn, catching all the strands together. Cut each loop, then trim them into desired shape. This one is in the form of a cone. Do not let this form a round ball, but keep one side flat to attach to hat. Make two smaller round balls of dark blue-green in the same manner and place one on either side of the cone-shaped henna ball. It takes about 5 yards of yarn for each ball. Do not spread the fingers for this size. This makes balls about 1 inch in diameter.

No. 7, yarn twist. The ornament between the peanuts is made a little differently. Take $2\frac{1}{2}$ yards of dark brown yarn and fold it into six lengths. Twist it, then tie a knot in the center. Make three more loose knots, tying one close to the other. Keep the twist in the yarn. Tack free ends together with thread. Begin with first knot, twist it once. Hold yarn in the hands and twist each knot. Tack them into a ball.

No. 8, chenille ornament. Near the center flower at top of crown make an ornament of nine strands of blue chenille. It requires 3 yards folded nine times, twisted and knotted as No. 7, except that the twists and knots are looser.

No. 9, sealing-wax leaf. Cut a piece of black buckram in the shape of a leaf, 2 inches long and $1\frac{3}{4}$ inches at the broadest point. Pierce hole in leaf and put in a wire and twist as for seeds and peanuts. Melt dark green sealing wax and put it on smooth side of buckram. Take long pin or needle and press into wax, making irregular effects. Place a little gold paint on leaf near stem and center. Make leaf on opposite side in same manner, only a lighter green. Attach both leaves to same stem and wind with mending tissue.

No. 10, yarn ornament. Make two ornaments as directed for No. 7. Use six strands of brown yarn for the larger. Place them at end of leaf. Make the smaller of four strands of lavender chenille, using three knots. Place this at side of leaf.

No. 11, yarn ornament. The small ball of blue yarn between the peanuts requires $2\frac{1}{2}$ yards. (See No. 6.) This time wind yarn around ends of two fingers held close together, thus making a smaller ball. Place dark peanut and one leaf on hat at the right of this ornament.

No. 12, yarn ornament. On left side of crown at base make a ball of green yarn shading to blue (turquoise) like No. 7. Place it next the green one. Attach stem of remaining peanut under green ball and into center on top of blue-green one. Extend ornament out on brim by bending.

No. 13, yarn ornament. Just above blue ball and at end of light green sealing-wax leaf, place a brown ornament. This will balance the brown ornament on the opposite side. Extending from under this ornament place a light green leaf and stem made as No. 2.

Any part of this trimming may be used. It is an excellent example of unusual color combination and will repay the effort expended on it. (See chapter i, "The Choice of a Hat.")

FLOWERS AND FRUIT

Almost every flower that grows has been reproduced at some time for millinery purposes. From the gaudy wreath for a child's hat to the most exquisitely fashioned French flowers are all gradations of material and workmanship. Berries, seeds, fruits, nuts, and vegetables are made in imitation of nature. Nuts and seeds are used in the natural form.

All sorts of materials are utilized—cambric, velvet, gauze, linen, silk, wool, chenille, leather, metal, and hand-carved wood.

The cost of flowers usually bears a direct relation to the artistic value. One rose may be three times the price of another. There is usually a legitimate reason for the difference. It may be evident to the connoisseur and entirely hidden from the unobservant. The materials in the higher-priced flower are proportionally better than in the cheap one. Fine choice of color and excellent modeling are the tests of beauty.

Flowers, whether hand or machine made, have a universal appeal. They suggest springtime and gaiety. As long as they give pleasure, few care how perishable they may be.

Velvet flower. Cut five petals by the pattern (Fig. 81, page 139) from chiffon or panne velvet, taking care that the pile runs from center to edge of petal. Cut five similar petals from taffeta for lining.

HANDMADE TRIMMINGS

With the edge of a hot iron vein the velvet petals as shown in Fig. 81. Start each time at lower point of petal. A heated hatpin may be used.

Prepare five loops of tie wire (Fig. 81), each long enough to extend from lower point of petal to within $\frac{3}{8}$ or $\frac{1}{2}$ inch of edge of petal (Fig. 81).

Glue taffeta linings to backs of velvet petals with wire loops between the two thicknesses of material. Use milliner's glue, applying it evenly to back of velvet.

When glue is dry, fold each petal lengthwise with velvet side in and steam lower half. Hold petal in left hand and when it is damp twist lower half of petal with right hand, making about three complete turns. Open petal and trim off frayed edges. Cut a small circle of velvet, $1\frac{3}{4}$ inches or larger in diameter, for center of flower. Stuff it with cotton fastened to a wire for stem and draw it up to form a ball. Fasten it in place with tie wire. Arrange sta-

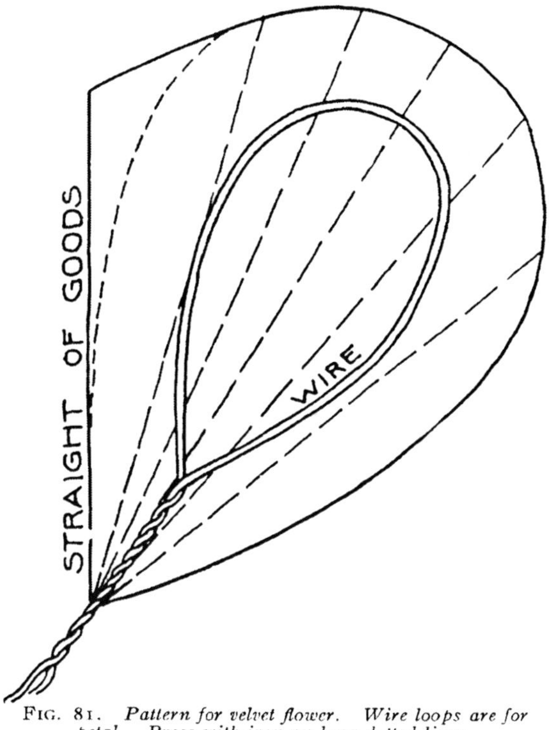

FIG. 81. *Pattern for velvet flower. Wire loops are for petal. Press with iron on long dotted lines. Cut on short dotted lines*

mens around this ball and again fasten them with tie wire. Then arrange petals around center, lapping curved side of each over straight side of adjoining petal. Fasten them in place with tie wire or needle and thread. Cover stem with mending tissue. Trim off underside of petals as indicated by dotted line (Fig. 81). This flower may be developed also in duvetyn.

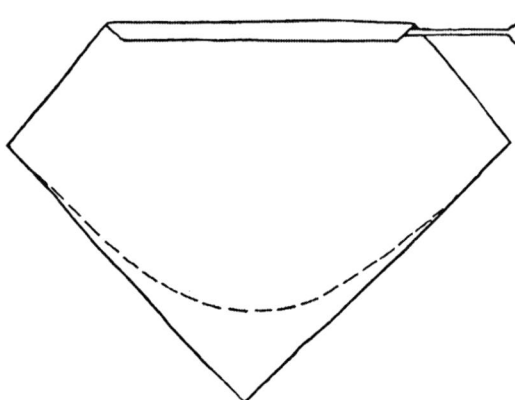

FIG. 82. *Silk flowers. Gather on dotted lines*

Silk flower. To make a flower that may be used for either hat or dress trimming, cut squares of silk any desired size; for example, five 4-inch squares. Insert long needle or hatpin into one corner of square and roll it toward center until roll meets diagonal, thus forming a triangle. Hold left-hand end of roll between third and fourth fingers of left hand; and right-hand end between thumb and first finger of left hand. Draw out hatpin and sew roll at right-hand end and gather the triangle (Fig. 82). Be sure to round lower point. Draw up thread and arrange petals around any center desired.

This flower may be made with as many as twelve or fifteen petals and from squares varying from 2 to 8 inches. When made large, this rose may be used as a corsage.

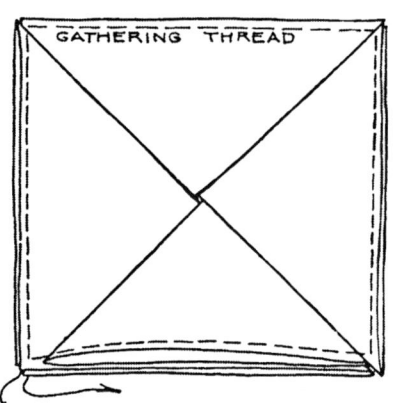

FIG. 83. *Futurist rose. Four squares arranged to form one square*

Futurist rose. Cut four squares of taffeta measuring from 2 to 5 inches. For the rose (Fig. 84, page 141) use 4½-inch squares.

HANDMADE TRIMMINGS 141

Fold squares diagonally, forming true bias, and pin edges together. Arrange the four squares to form one square the same size as the single square of taffeta, having bias edges folded under each other (Fig. 83, page 140). Gather edges and draw them up tightly around a center piece and fasten them by sewing through and through the gathers. The center may be several small circles of contrasting color stuffed with cotton and arranged on wires to form stems; or it may be one large circle stuffed with cotton to form a ball; or it may be a bunch of stamens fastened with tie wire. To finish, fold edge of each petal back $\frac{3}{8}$ inch.

Leaves. Take 2- or 3-inch squares of taffeta, according to the size desired. Fold the square to form a triangle. Fold extreme points of triangle toward worker, letting them meet lower point of triangle, which will be stem end of leaf, thus forming a square one-half the size of the original square. Now fold the two outer points of square twice toward the center and fasten them with wire, which forms the stem. The wire may be covered by winding with yarn, mending tissue, taffeta, or chenille.

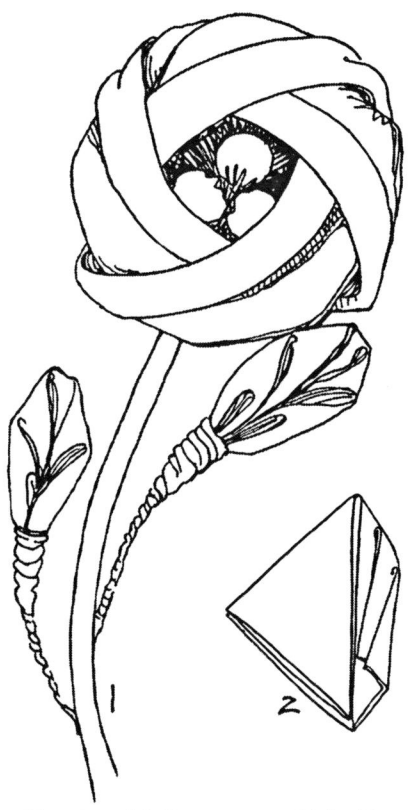

FIG. 84. (1) *Futurist rose;* (2) *leaf in making*

Poppy. Velvet or silk may be used. This flower is used for the decoration of hats and is most attractive for a corsage on an evening gown.

Making petal (Fig. 85, below). Cut four petals of velvet, and sew wire around edge of each petal with blanket or buttonhole stitch. Turn edge to wrong side and make a small hem, being careful not to let stitches show. Or put glue on edge and turn back, forming a hem. The latter method is satisfactory if careful work is done.

Making center. Cut circle 2 inches in diameter and gather edge. Prepare piece of cotton to stuff center, by winding piece of lace wire around center of cotton (Fig. 86, No. 1). Cut required length for stem. Bring ends of cotton to center so as to make a soft pad over the wire. Pull velvet down over cotton to see if padding is full enough. It must be stuffed very full. Draw gathering thread and sew velvet in place (Fig. 86, No. 2). Place a bunch of stamens at back of ball. Leave them intact with the wire around the center, spread, and sew them all around center from underside.

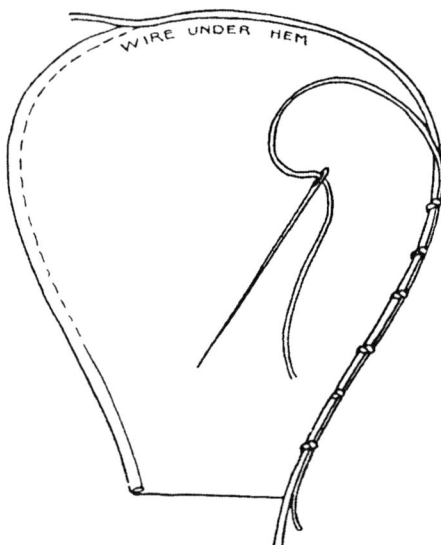

FIG. 85. *Poppy pattern and wiring*

Sewing petals. Crush ends of petals and sew them to stem under center pad. Sew second petal opposite first, then third and fourth in the same manner. Cover stem with chenille, floss, yarn, ribbon, mending tissue, or material cut in strips.

This flower may be made by cutting for each petal two pieces of taffeta, or one piece of taffeta and one piece of duvetyn. Stitch the two petals together on the wrong side. Sew wire to seam. Turn the petal and proceed to make flower as previously described. Or picot edges together, omitting wire, then finish as above.

HANDMADE TRIMMINGS

Buttonmold flower. An attractive trimming may be made with wooden buttonmolds, a scrap of velvet, a piece of silk, and a short length of yarn (Fig. 76, No. 6, page 131). To make,

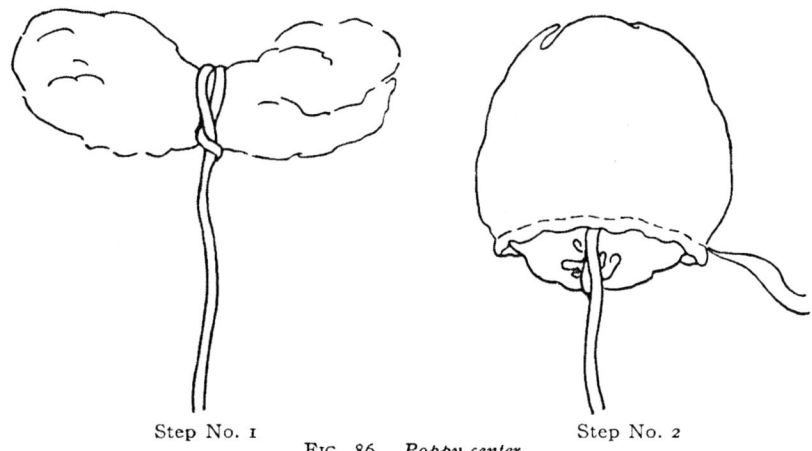

Step No. 1   Step No. 2
FIG. 86. *Poppy center*

cover bottonmold with a circle of silk or velvet. Cut material about ½ inch larger. Gather cut edge and slip circle over mold, drawing it together on the back. In the center, make decorative stitches of yarn. These may be either cross-stitch or outline, or a combination of the two. The stitch may be applied to material after mold is covered.

Band upturned or collar on edge. Cut bias strip of silk or satin the circumference of botton plus seam. Be careful not to take the measurement too closely. For width of bias strip measure and cut diameter of mold plus ½ to 1 inch. Join bias seam, forming a circle. Fold width through middle and gather cut edge. Place this piece around mold so folded edge will stand up.

Daisy. *Material.* Ribbon, flower centers, tie wire, and cotton. The length of ribbon required depends upon its width. The daisy shown in Fig. 87, page 144, requires 16 inches of No. 7 ribbon. With a knot in the thread, begin at selvage near cut end of ribbon and run row of stitches to meet point ½ inch from cut edge on opposite selvage. Gather along selvage for 1¾ inches and slant stitches to a point 3 inches from starting point on first selvage. This forms one petal. Continue as shown in illustration, leaving 1 inch between inner edge and 3 inches between outer edge of each petal.

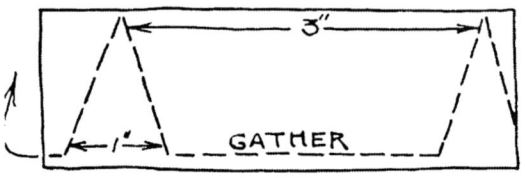

FIG. 87. *Detail for daisy petal*

Gather five petals and draw gathering thread very tight to form flower. Sew cut edges together.

To make center, use small circle of silk gathered around edge and stuffed with cotton. The cotton may be attached to wire first if a stem is desired. If stem is used, slip wire through hole in center of petals and fasten petals to it with tie wire. Bring it over and alternate between petals, hiding the wire in their folds. Daisy centers may be purchased and used instead of silk if preferred.

Tailored rose. *Materials.* Two-inch circle of crinoline or flexible net, cotton for padding, taffeta, satin, organdy, or velvet.

Making. Place a small wad of cotton in center of circle of crinoline and cover it with 2-inch square of taffeta, sewing at outer edges to hold it in place. This may be a contrasting color if desired. Cut ten bias strips, 3 inches wide and 4 inches long. Fold

FIG. 88. *Tailored rose*

them lengthwise through middle and place them over top of circle. Fold three strips over top, one overlapping the other, showing center slightly. Fold cut edge of material to back of circle and fasten it first with pins to try the effect, then sew it in place. Put remaining petals on as illustrated in Fig. 88. Number of petals depends upon size of flower desired. Sometimes the petals are arranged in uneven formation. To give a more tailored effect, arrange them evenly.

Grapes. *Materials.* Velvet, silk, satin, or a combination of silk of a brilliant hue covered with contrasting color of georgette, chiffon, or any transparent material. A red or purple silk covered with navy blue georgette makes an attractive combination.

Making. Cut 2-inch square of material and gather it around edge to form circle. Do not trim corners. Draw gathers a little and stuff material with cotton, then draw up tight and press with fingers to make ball slightly oval. With heavy silk or mercerized floss take a stitch through grape at gathering thread. Wind floss around grape from gathering thread to points of square to form a stem, then fasten it with one or two stitches, leaving end of thread with needle attached. Make a second grape in same manner, attaching to same piece of floss. Take stitch in the grape and wind floss around as above. Do not cut threads. Make third grape separately as for the first, then fasten the three together, being careful to leave ends of threads to each or every two grapes. To form the large bunch, crochet a number of the small bunches together.

Leaves. Make each leaf of velvet. Cut foundation shape of black crinoline. With milliner's glue attach velvet to crinoline, then cut velvet, following the outline. Silk may be pasted to the back in the same manner.

To vein the leaf, use either hot wire or needle on top of velvet; or press the leaf, using edge of iron. Crush one-half of leaf by steaming and twisting it to make imprints in the velvet.

Organdy flowers. The chief charm of organdy flowers lies in the subtle combination of colors. Any small scrap of organdy is useful. Yellow and green stamens, tie wire, and brown mending tissue are needed. To make one type of flower (bell flower) see Fig. 90, page 147.

Picot the straight edge of organdy on one side. If more than one flower of the same color is to be made, cut a strip of organdy 3 inches wide and 8½ inches long. Hemstitch through middle of piece lengthwise, making two strips 1½ inches wide by 8½ inches long. The length may be from 6 to 8½ inches. Roll and whip ends of strips together, using thread the color of the organdy. Fold picot edge to right side, about ¼ inch, and gather it very near the folded edge. Draw to desired size and tack it in place. The opening should be comparatively small. With a double thread gather lower or cut edge of material preparatory to inserting center.

Mix yellow and green stamens and choose a suitable number (two bunches will make three flowers). Measure and cut about

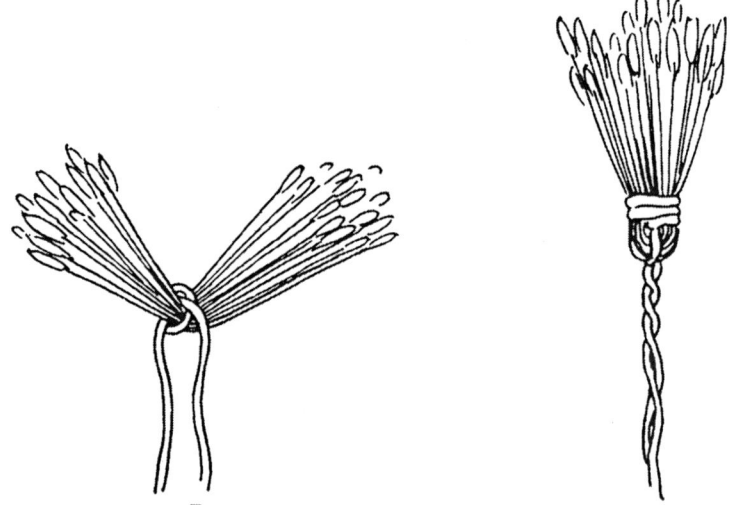

FIG. 89. *Bell flower — stamens wired*

10 inches of tie wire. Twist wire tightly around center stamens, beginning at middle of 10-inch piece. Fold stamens, bringing

HANDMADE TRIMMINGS 147

all pollen ends together, and twist one end of wire around base of stamens once or twice; then bring the two wires together to form the stems by twisting two or three times (Fig. 89). Crush stamens down a little to overcome stiffness.

Putting center and organdy together. Place prepared center down through gathered organdy flower from top. Draw bottom gathering thread tight with gathering thread. If this is done, the organdy will not pull off. The center must extend slightly above top of the organdy (Fig. 90).

Leaves. Picot edge in a straight strip as for the flower. Cut strip 1½ inches wide and 3 inches long.

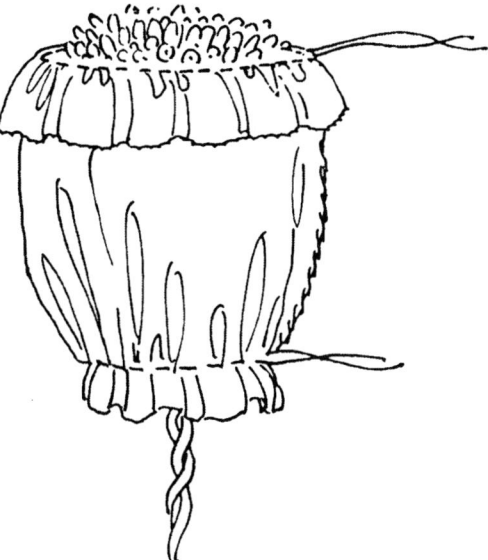

FIG. 90. *Bell flower — finishing flower*

Making leaf. Fold leaf as if mitering a corner, making a pointed end (Fig. 91). The picoted edge follows fold of material on each side, making a square corner. Gather or make small plaits at lower edge of leaf. Take a 10-inch piece of tie wire, begin at center of wire and wrap it tightly around end of leaf, then draw the two pieces of wire together and wrap one around the other, making the stem (Fig. 92).

Bud. Cut 2½-inch square of plain organdy (not hemstitched). Fold square in half to form rectangle, then fold over each side of folded edge to meet in center of rectangle, thus forming a triangle. Fold triangle through center (Fig. 91, page 148). Wrap wire around bottom as for leaf and twist it to form bud (Fig. 92).

Tendril. Use green wire which was wrapped around flower centers. Wind wire around a large darning needle to give a spiral

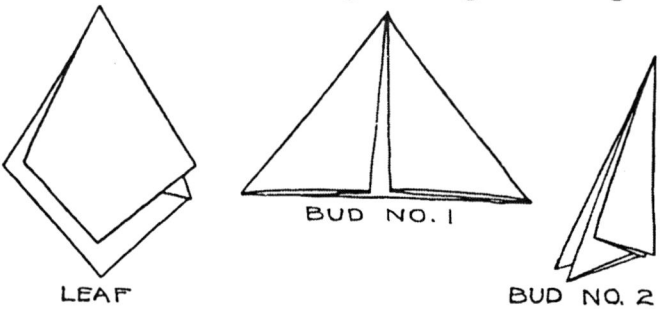

FIG. 91. *Leaf and bud for bell flower*

effect. Attach a tie wire to lengthen the tendril (Fig. 92). White wire may be dyed if green wire is not available.

Wrapping stems. Cut mending tissue in narrow strips, begin at base of flower, and wrap each stem separately. In grouping flowers wrap the bunch after the flowers are placed together.

To make other types of organdy flowers. The following flowers may be made from organdy, georgette, or silk (Fig. 93). Georgette is preferable.

Using a thimble or any smooth tubular implement, bring tie wire around it and twist ends to secure circle. Ends of tie wires should be left long enough to form the stem (Fig. 94). Cut

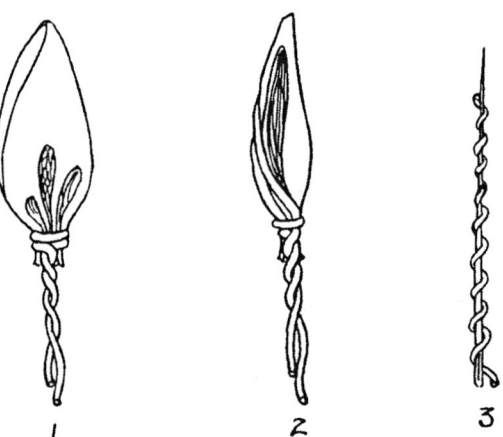

FIG. 92. (1) *Leaf of bell flower;* (2) *bud of bell flower;* (3) *tendril of bell flower*

five $2\frac{1}{2}$-inch circles for a 1-inch petal. Fold square diagonally and slip circle of tie wire between folds. Draw corners of square

HANDMADE TRIMMINGS 149

to center on stem part of tie-wire circle and fasten them in place with an extra piece of tie wire. Make five petals and arrange

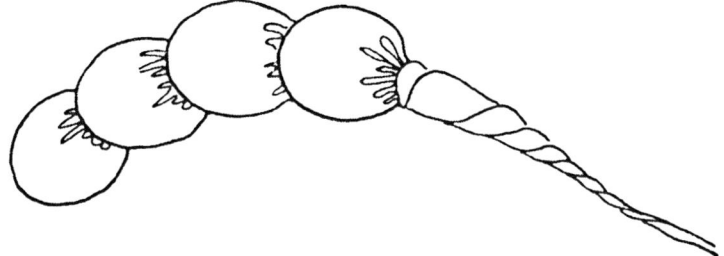

FIG. 93. *Georgette petals*

them around some stamens attached to a piece of tie wire. One side of each petal should overlap the adjoining petal with the roll turning outward. Secure them firmly by winding tie wire around petal, then bend petals any shape desired and cover stem with mending tissue.

If georgette is used, it is advisable to color tie wire by dipping the circle in dye. This often changes the effect of the whole flower, as wire shows through plainly. Buds and leaves may be added. The petals may be arranged in many different ways and may be large or small as desired. One attractive arrangement is shown in Fig. 93. The same design may be developed in black maline over silver or gold wire. If the petals are larger, the decoration is suitable for dress trimmings or hair ornaments.

FIG. 94. *Wire frame for georgette petals*

Metallic novelty fabrics give a good effect in making various types of flowers and fruits.

Another flower may be made from organdy. Cut all petals from true bias strips.

MEASUREMENTS

Center.................................$1\frac{1}{2}$-inch circle
2 petals..............................$2\frac{3}{4}$ inches by $1\frac{1}{2}$ inches
3 petals..............................$3\frac{3}{4}$ inches by 2 inches
3 petals..............................5 inches by $2\frac{1}{2}$ inches

Roll upper edge of each petal and gather it along sides (Fig. 95), being sure to round corners and leave points projecting so as to give more material for attaching petal to stems.

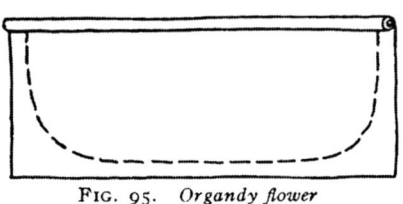

FIG. 95. *Organdy flower*

Gather the 1½-inch circle and draw it up over a small ball of padding cotton, which should be attached to a piece of tie wire long enough to form a stem. Stamens may be used around the organdy center or they may be used instead of the organdy center.

Arrange petals around center, placing two smallest petals first, then the three of next size, and lastly, the three largest ones, sewing each in place. Wrap stem with mending tissue, organdy, or yarn.

Still another organdy flower may be made as follows. Five 3-inch squares make two flowers. Fold squares diagonally and cut through bias fold. Roll bias edge. Gather organdy along straight edge, and round the point. Draw out each petal and arrange it around desired center, which must be fastened to a tie-wire stem. Let each petal overlap the adjoining one. This may have more petals added if desired. Wind stem with mending tissue, organdy, or yarn. Buds and leaves may be added.

Yarn flower No. 1. *Materials.* Yarn, silk or artificial silk floss, chenille or any embroidery floss; knitting needle or pencil, size depending upon result desired; tie wire of any length.

Fasten yarn or floss to knitting needle with a slip loop. Bend tie wire in half and slip wire through yarn loop so that a single strand of wire hangs on each side of loop in yarn. Cross tie wire (Fig. 96).

Bring long end of yarn around needle from back to front and again cross tie wire over yarn. This will form two loops of yarn on the needle and produce a little ridge of wire which holds the

HANDMADE TRIMMINGS

loops together. Continue until desired number of loops are formed, then slip them off the needle and arrange them in any form desired (Fig. 98, Nos. 1, 2, page 153). The loops may be cut after being removed from needle, thus giving a fuzzy design (Fig. 98, No. 3).

Yarn flower No. 2. On heavy cardboard make a circle from 2 to 5 inches in diameter, depending on the size of the flower. Divide circumference of circle in eight equal parts and notch edge (Fig. 97, below). About 7 yards of yarn are required for a 5-inch circle. Any size of yarn may be used.

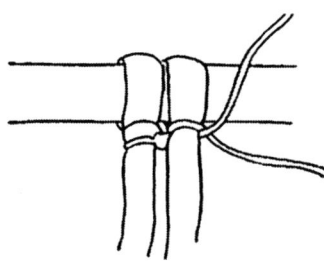

FIG. 96. *Yarn flower No. 1*

Thread a needle and put it through the center of circle, leaving about 3 inches of yarn on the underside. Wind the yarn around notches from 1 to 2, across to 6, then 5. Now hold the yarn with the thumb at the center and cross to 4 and 3, then back to 7 and 8. Return to center and catch down yarn which has been held in place. Work from left to right, bringing needle under each succeeding line. When taking a stitch, be careful to point needle toward outer edge of circle,

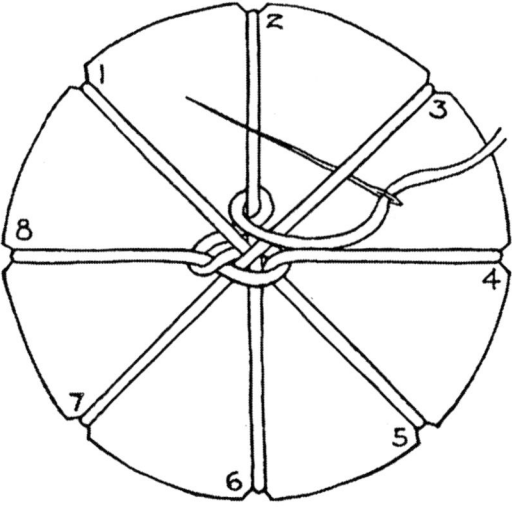

FIG. 97. *Yarn flower No. 2*

forming a backstitch over each vein. Fill space between center and outer edge. Remove stitches from notches and pull thread that has been used in making the stitches, thus forming flower. By adjusting the stitches along the veins—i. e., pushing them toward or pulling them away from the center—you may produce different effects. The flower may be turned inside out, showing the ribbed or veined side (Fig. 98, Nos. 4, 5, 6, page 153). See "Crocheted Flower" for suggestions for stem and leaves.

Crocheted flower. The flower motif popular in Irish crochet furnishes a good example for hat trimmings. Directions for making such flowers may be found in many booklets on needlework (Fig. 98, No. 7, page 153). Angora yarn or chenille has a more interesting texture than plain yarn.

Making flower. Crochet five stitches, connect to make a circle. Make ten single crochet stitches over this circle. Around this circle make five loops, each loop containing three chain stitches. Catch each one to circle with single crochet. Fill each loop with five double crochets and catch the last of each group down with a single crochet.

Make next row in same manner, but take seven stitches for each loop instead of five. Continue until flower is finished.

Stem. Make stem by folding three or four pieces of tie wire together. Single crochet over the wire or wind wire with yarn (Fig. 98). Lace wire or cord may be used for stem.

Leaf. Crochet the number of stitches desired for length of leaf. Double crochet on both sides of chain and attach it to stem with three or four single crochet stitches. A smaller leaf may be made by use of double crochet on one side of stitches made for length of leaf. If a point is desired at end, finish with one or two crochet stitches. Or make the regular Irish crochet leaf.

Straw flowers and leaves. Attractive trimmings may be made from plain or fancy straw braid by drawing the thread in edge of the straw to form various-shaped petals and leaves. Horsehair braid is particularly adapted to use for such ornaments.

Fig. 98. *Crocheted yarn trimmings*
Nos. 1, 2, 3, variations of Fig. 96
Nos. 4, 5, 6, variations of Fig. 97
No. 7. crocheted flower

For the illustration below, Fig. 99, ¾ yard of straw 1 inch wide is needed for the petals of the flower. Each petal will measure about 5½ inches. Do not cut them apart. Shape petals by drawing thread on runner edge of straw. Arrange them around a central point and fasten them with wire. The center of the flower may be made of contrasting straw, which may be formed into a ball or raveled out and tied with wire to give a more ragged appearance.

Form leaves by folding straw, but do not draw the thread. Cut each leaf separately. Frame wire may be used for the stem and covered with straw, yarn, or chenille. Arrange flower and leaves as desired.

Made quill. This is an attractive form of trimming. It is more decorative and less severe than a feather. The outline or proportions may vary according to taste. In general, it conforms to the shape of a natural feather.

Making. Use crinoline or buckram for the foundation. Sew frame wire through center to form rib of quill. Cover both

FIG. 99. *Straw trimmings*

sides of foundation with velvet, silk, cloth, or leather. Paste the material with milliner's glue. Trim and leave the cut edges or decorate in any way desired. Bind with ribbon, braid, or

HANDMADE TRIMMINGS 155

decorative stitches in yarn, raffia, or chenille. The wire may extend beyond the end of the quill and be wrapped with yarn or material. The entire wire may be covered and attached

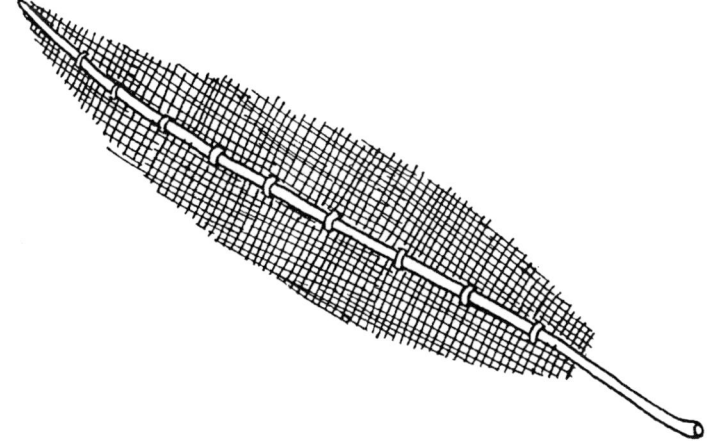

FIG. 100. *Foundation for made quill*

to outside of quill for decorative effect. Bend the quill in any desired shape.

Ribbon plaiting. Any kind of ribbon may be used for this form of band trimming. The design in Fig. 75, No. 5, page 131, shows ribbon about 1 inch wide. Make by folding into a series of inverted box plaits alternating with two side plaits. Catch the edges of box plaits together as in illustration. Variations are possible in the spacing and depth of plaits.

CHAPTER XIV

DECORATIVE STITCHES AND PROCESSES

Appliqué — Blanket Stitch — Catch Stitch — Catstitch — Chain Stitch — Couching Stitch — Crocheting — Cross-Stitch — Darning — French Knots — Herringbone Stitch — Knot or Snail Stitch, or Running Chain — Lazy-Daisy Stitch — Leaf Stitch — Outline, Crewel, or Stem Stitch — Satin Stitch — Seed Stitch — Use of Stitches

Appliqué. Appliqué is a form of decoration in which pieces of cloth are sewed to a background to form a design. Bits of cloth in contrasting color may be applied by hemming or stitching over the trimmed edge with couching, chain, outline, blanket, or other decorative stitches. Appliqué may be used on hats very effectively when a flat trimming is desired.

Blanket stitch. This stitch may be worked either from left to right or from right to left, but preference is given to the former method. Hold lower edge of material to be finished toward worker. Make depth and spacing of stitches according to the effect desired. Begin near outer edge and take two or three running stitches toward edge. This will fasten thread without use of knot. Put needle in at starting point and take single stitch over edge, allowing needle to pass through loop formed by thread. Space stitches evenly $\frac{1}{4}$ or $\frac{1}{2}$ inch apart, or any other distance desired, allowing the needle to pass through the loop each time, thus forming a continuous line on edge of material. To add interest, group the stitches in twos and threes, making some long and some short. When made open and irregular the blanket stitch may be combined with darning stitch, French knots, etc. Contrasting colors offer opportunity for many variations. Used for finishing edges and as a decoration for trimming (Fig. 101).

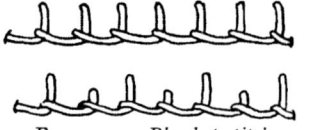

Fig. 101. *Blanket stitch*

DECORATIVE STITCHES AND PROCESSES

Catch stitch. (See page 91, Fig. 50.)

Catstitch. (See page 91, Fig. 51.)

Chain stitch. Place work over left forefinger. Point needle toward worker. Space stitches long or short as desired. Hold thread down with left thumb each time a stitch is taken. Insert needle where the last stitch came out, fastening loop down (Fig. 102).

FIG. 102. *Chain stitch*

Couching stitch. The couching stitch is a simple form of outlining. Lay a thread down on the cloth (usually a heavy thread or two or three threads). Fasten this in any outline desired with a smaller thread or with a group of stitches forming a decoration. Take a small stitch across the heavy thread at right angles or slanting. These stitches may be grouped in twos or threes with spaces between them (Fig. 103).

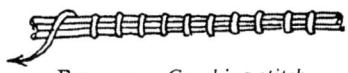

FIG. 103. *Couching stitch*

Crocheting. This may be employed in novelty trimmings. Since there are many patterns given in women's magazines and booklets on crocheting, directions for stitches are not included here (Fig. 98, No. 7, page 153).

Cross-stitch. When employed on hats cross-stitch is usually a free-hand decoration. Make this stitch by carrying one slant stitch across another at right angles. All the upper stitches run in the same direction (Fig. 104).

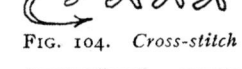

FIG. 104. *Cross-stitch*

Darning. Any straight-line design may be carried out in darning stitches. They may be evenly spaced, or if preferred the surface may be covered by irregular stitches (Fig. 105).

FIG. 105. *Darning stitch*

French knots. Use heavy thread. Fasten with a knot on wrong side of material. Hold thread down with left thumb. Put needle under thread from right to left. Turn needle from left to right, twisting thread. Insert needle near where it came out of cloth. Pull thread close around needle. Bring needle out at next point for a French knot (Fig. 106).

Herringbone stitch. See catstitch.

FIG. 106. *French knots*

FIG. 107. *Knot or snail stitch*

Knot or snail stitch, or running chain. The thread is fastened at intervals by a knot stitch which is a form of chain stitch. Hold thread down with left thumb. Insert needle at left of thread. Throw thread in a loop. This ties a knot on surface of cloth. Space knots regularly or irregularly, close or far apart (Fig. 107).

Lazy-daisy stitch. Separated chain, loop, or teardrop stitch. This may be made in the form of flower petals. If made in a straight line or for separated spots, it is called *separated chain*, or *teardrop*. It is merely a single chain stitch fastened down at the outer edge of the loop (Fig. 108).

FIG. 108. *Lazy-daisy stitch*

Leaf stitch. This is similar to featherstitch. Begin near point of leaf, make two or three stitches toward point. Then place needle in point of leaf and bring it out about $\frac{1}{4}$ or $\frac{1}{2}$ inch below point. Take each stitch from sides to center, holding thread with thumb so that needle passes over thread. Carry thread continuously as in featherstitch. Bring to center each time to make veining. The stitches may vary in slant and spacing to produce many effects (Fig. 109).

FIG. 109. *Leaf stitch*

Outline, crewel, or stem stitch. Work from left to right or over left forefinger away from worker. Bring needle up, take a stitch forward, then halfway back to left of first stitch. Continue overlapping the stitches in this way (Fig. 110). A slender line or a thick effect may be produced by less or

DECORATIVE STITCHES AND PROCESSES

more overlapping. This may cover a surface as well as an outline.

Satin stitch. The satin stitch is used to cover surfaces. It is the same on both sides. It is merely an over-and-over stitch and is used for embroidering dots, leaves, petals, or any other solid design (Fig. 111).

FIG. 110. *Outline stitch*

Seed stitch. This is often more attractive than French knots and is used in the same way. It depends upon the thickness of the thread whether one, two, or more stitches should be piled upon each other. Run needle under cloth from one seed stitch to another (Fig. 112).

FIG. 111. *Satin stitch*

Use of stitches. Any one of these simple stitches may be changed by the spacing; for example, feather-stitch may suggest a solid, broad leaf or a fine line. Many stitches may be combined to form new designs.

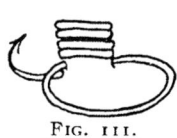

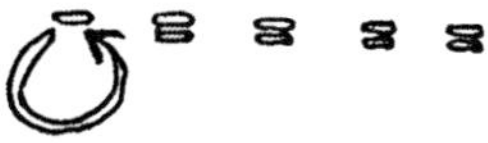

FIG. 112. *Seed stitch*

It is possible to produce a great variety of surface effects with the same material and color in different stitches or by varying the color and the material.

Striking differences are shown in wool yarn, mercerized cotton, metallic thread, rayon (artificial silk), and chenille.

CHAPTER XV

FEATHERS

LAWS GOVERNING USE OF FEATHERS

KINDS OF FEATHERS: Aigret or Egret—Aigrette—Barnyard Fowls—Duck—Goose—Gourah—Grebe—Guinea Fowl—Heron—Marabou—Numidi—Ostrich—Paradise—Parrot and Parrakeet—Peacock—Pheasant—Quill—Tip—Turkey—Vulture—Willow Plume

The use of feathers, like that of all other hat trimmings, is seasonal and subject to changes in fashion. The form in which the feather trimming is applied varies also. Plumes and tips closely curled may be used one year; the next season there may be a demand for willow plumes, and the following year, one for pompons or ostrich band trimming. Feathers may be treated so as to give a variety of effects; for example, burnt ostrich (flues removed) and glycerin ostrich (shiny surface).

As a matter of fact, some form of ostrich is always on the market.

Small birds are in vogue from time to time. Again, only wings, breasts, or quills are popular. Many wings and breasts are manufactured from loose feathers.

LAWS GOVERNING USE OF FEATHERS

Certain rare imported feathers are not allowed on the American market.

The sale of paradise, goura, and egret (aigrette) is prohibited by law. The large demand for the plumage threatened to exterminate the species, because the finest feathers were taken from the birds while they were caring for their young. This resulted in the death of the mother bird and the young birds perished from starvation. Through the efforts of the National Association of the Audubon Society the propagation of these birds is assured.

FEATHERS

Some beautiful birds, like the Chinese pheasant, have been imported and are protected by state laws.

All of the states have laws protecting all of the wild birds except a few of the hawk species and some others of minor importance. Also there are United States laws to protect them while in transit. A decision of the Treasury Department penalizes the possessor of aigrettes and paradise feathers so that the wearer may have them confiscated at any time.

KINDS OF FEATHERS

The following birds furnish feathers which are fashionable from time to time:

Aigret or egret (pr. ā′ gret or ē′ gret). From the white heron, which furnishes delicate sweeping feathers. Sale prohibited in United States.

Aigrette. A tuft of feathers; also called "osprey." Sale prohibited in United States.

Barnyard fowls. Supply wings and quills dyed or used in natural color. Most of the wings and birds are made from the feathers of barnyard fowls.

Spanish Coq. A kind of aigrette. The shaded tail feathers of the cock. *Hackle* comes from the long slender feathers on the sides of the cock.

Duck. Wild ducks have beautiful colors on wings and breasts. Therefore these parts were formerly used as trimmings. Wild ducks are very generally protected by state laws during certain seasons.

Goose. Feathers may be used for wings, breasts, bands, pompons, and aigrettes. Most goose feathers have been treated and are known as *burnt goose*.

Gourah. A species of pigeon known as the crown pigeon. The feathers are delicate and rather short. The plain gray is from the female; the blue with white markings, from the male. Sale prohibited in United States.

Grebe. A sea bird without curly feathers. Used for breasts and band trimmings.

Guinea fowl. Speckled gray bird which furnishes wings, breasts, and band trimmings.

Heron. See *Aigret*. Called numidi.

Marabou. An African stork whose soft, white down from tail and wings is used for making trimming. Usually made into banding and pompons.

Numidi. Feathers from the Numidian crane, a bird which resembles the heron. One species called blue crane, or blue heron. Sale prohibited in United States.

Ostrich. A native of Africa and Arabia. Now bred on farms in Africa, California, and Florida. The female is gray and the male black with wings and tail bordered in white. Feathers are plucked at certain seasons of the year. They are dyed, finished, and made into plumes, tips, pompons, and band trimmings.

Paradise. Native of New Guinea. The male has peculiar gorgeous plumage. Tufts of feathers generally grow from beneath the wings. These tufts seem to fall in a shower from the whole body. The body of the birds may be brown, red or gray with different colored plumage. The combination most commonly seen is a red-brown body with orange plumage. Sale prohibited in United States.

Parrot and parrakeet. The natural undyed feathers are used for making wings and breasts.

Peacock. Native of the tropics but raised in Europe and America. Brilliantly marked tail feathers used as an aigrette and for band trimming.

Pheasant. Introduced into the United States from Asia and Europe. The male bird has brilliant plumage. Feathers used in natural colors, dyed, or burnt with acid. They are made into wings, breasts, and long tail effects. Of the many species, the golden pheasant is most prized for plumage.

FEATHERS

Partridge and grouse are closely related to the pheasant and their feathers may be used in the same way, subject to state game laws.

Quill. Stiff feather from tail or wing of large bird.

Tip. A short ostrich feather taken from the wing of the bird. It is smaller than a plume and is usually curled tightly.

Turkey. Wing and tail feathers may be used in the natural color or dyed.

Vulture. A large bird of prey whose wing feathers make handsome quills. The soft feathers are often treated with acid and glycerin and used for aigrette effects.

Willow plume. This form of ostrich trimming is sometimes used. It is made by tying flues end to end on a plume. This enlarges the plume and gives it a graceful sweep. Willow plumes may be manufactured chemically.

CHAPTER XVI

HAT LININGS

DIRECTIONS FOR MAKING: No. 1, Plain Lining—No. 2, Tailored Lining—No. 3, French Lining

Hat linings may be bought ready-made or prepared at home. They are usually made of silk or mercerized cotton materials in black or white. A silk hat may be lined with the same material of which it is made. There are three types of hat linings:

No. 1, plain lining. A strip of thin material sewed to the headsize is gathered with a draw-string.

No. 2, tailored lining. The cap crown gives a tailored effect. It is entirely finished and then attached to the headsize.

No. 3, French lining. A cap effect made by gathering the edge of a circular piece of material and attaching it to a wire. It is used chiefly in transparent hats.

DIRECTIONS FOR MAKING

No. 1, plain lining. Cut a straight or bias piece of silk approximately 2 inches longer than the headsize and about 6 inches wide. (It should be the height of the crown plus $2\frac{1}{2}$ inches.) Make a hem $\frac{1}{2}$ inch wide on one side and insert No. 1 ribbon the length of the lining. Do not draw up the ribbon until later.

To attach lining, hold hat on knee and work from right to left. Begin at back and place right side of lining next to brim. Fold back one end of lining $\frac{1}{2}$ inch and place cut edge of lining down into the headsize about $\frac{1}{2}$ inch. Take a small stitch or two (one directly over the other), with the needle at right angles to the headsize. Hold lining lightly with left hand. Take next stitch about $\frac{1}{2}$ inch from first. After sewing lining around headsize lap one end over the other and slip-stitch the two together.

HAT LININGS

Do not sew through the hem and ribbon. This lining may be made by sewing the ends in a seam and inserting the ribbon through a buttonhole in the hem at the center front. Otherwise it is the same.

For the tip, cut a 5- or 6-inch square of material and paste or tack the corners lightly to the tip of the crown. (It is on this piece that the designer's name is often found.) Draw up the ribbon and tie it, taking care not to make the lining too tight.

No. 2, tailored lining. (This kind of lining may be bought ready-made.) Cut a bias strip of material the length and width as directed above. Join the seam and press it. Cut an ellipse 4 by 6 inches of crinoline or mull. Cut and baste to this foundation a piece of the lining material. Divide the bias strip in quarters and gather it on one side. Divide the ellipse, pin the two right sides together, baste, and stitch. See previous instructions for sewing lining to hat (lining No. 1).

A small bias-covered cord may be inserted in this seam before stitching, or a small cord may be sewed on to cover the seam.

No. 3, French lining. For transparent crowns make this lining of maline, chiffon, georgette, or organdy.

Measure the diameter of crown from base over tip to base on opposite side as directed in measurements for one-piece crown, and make a pattern. Cut a circle $\frac{1}{2}$ inch larger than the pattern. Measure and cut a piece of wire to fit inside of headsize and join ends of wire with a clamp. Fold edge of material over wire $\frac{1}{2}$ inch and sew it with running stitches. Gather fullness in place. Pin wire to headsize and tack it in place. Take care not to reduce size of crown by making wire too small.

PART VI. RENOVATION AND CARE OF HAT

CHAPTER XVII

RENOVATION AND CARE

HANDLING THE HAT
GENERAL UPKEEP OR CARE
FRESHENING STRAW HATS
RESHAPING FRAMES
VARYING THE STYLE OF CROWN

RENOVATING MATERIALS: To Steam Velvet—To Make Panne or Mirror Velvet—To Make Brocade or Broadtail Velvet—To Clean Ribbon—To Tint Flowers—To Improve Worn Feathers—To Clean Lace—To Tint Lace—To Clean Black Lace—To Clean Gold and Silver Lace—To Freshen Veils

HANDLING THE HAT

The trained milliner has developed a method of handling which prevents misshaping of frames and soiling of materials. She is sensitive to the things that injure hats. This feeling for the knowledge of how to handle hats comes through experience. Nevertheless, everyone should at least know how to pick up a hat and pack it away properly. When placing it on the head, use both hands in such a manner that there will be no strain or pull on any part of the frame of the hat. Do not lift a hat by the brim, but slip the hand under the crown. Hats are packed in the shops so as to rest on rolls of tissue paper. If the same care is used in the home, hats will retain their freshness longer.

GENERAL UPKEEP OR CARE

A new hat proclaims the fact by its fresh, unhandled look. There are no loose feathers, frayed or faded flowers, rain spots, or general signs of rustiness. To keep a hat in this condition requires attention to a few details. A carefully brushed hat may even be exposed to the rain and not become rusty. It takes only a moment to tack a piece of trimming in place, trim the petals of a flower or edge of a wing, apply a bit of glue to a feather, or veil a breast with maline. The time so spent is well paid for in the appearance of the renovated hat. If only a part of the trimming needs replacing, it is advisable to remove all of it and clean and renovate the hat before trimming it.

FRESHENING STRAW HATS

Brush the hat well to remove dust and cover it with a coat of dye of the same color or darker, or give it a coat of lacquer. If neither of these is available, use ordinary black shoe polish. Black straw can be freshened by brushing with alcohol. Black chip or Milan straw may be oiled with vaseline, glycerin, or olive oil put on with a flannel cloth. After oiling give the braid a coat of clear shellac.

Leghorn or Panama hats may be sent to a professional cleaner or done at home as follows: Scrub the hat with soap and water and wipe with a wet cloth and then with a dry one. Stuff the crown with paper or cloth and press it, holding the hat by the padding. Press flat brims on the edge of a board and curved ones over a pad held in the hand. Always press with a cloth over the straw. If the brim of a straw hat is too large, a few rows of braid may be removed and the edge finished with one or more rows of ornamental braid or with bias folds of silk or velvet.

The brim of a Leghorn hat may be altered as follows: Cut off brim where desired, dampen the edge, turn it under, and press. Face brim with silk or velvet or finish the edge with ornamental braid or bias folds. (See chapters ix and xi.)

To reshape any straw, first dampen it and shape it with the hands and press as directed above, then shellac.

To bleach straw hats use a solution of weak oxalic acid, lemon juice, or peroxide of hydrogen. Rinse and dry the hat in the sun.

RESHAPING FRAMES

If the general shape of the frame is to be changed, remove headsize and edge wire. If the headsize is too large, cut the brim through the middle, from front to back, and overlap it to desired size and sew. If the headsize is small, measure and cut a wire the desired size, place it over the hat, and sew it in place. Slash and finish the headsize as directed on page 44.

If edge of brim is too large, trim it to desired size. If small, add stiff material, such as buckram or willow, to edge of brim. If a drooping or upturning brim is desired, slash the brim from edge to headsize, overlap it slightly, and sew it in place. The number of slashes depends upon the shape desired. Cover each of the overlapped pieces with a bias strip of crinoline or muslin on both sides of brim. Wire edge and bind as directed on page 45.

If the frame has become broken, or is out of shape, it can be made to look almost like new by removal of all the covering. Dampen the frame and press it with an iron. A roll of cloth or paper must be held under a rolled brim or crown while pressing is being done unless a tommy iron is convenient. This iron is so small that it will take care of all the little intricate curves in hats without difficulty. If the frame is broken, a piece of crinoline may be sewed over the broken place and pressed. The frame is then ready for covering.

VARYING THE STYLE OF CROWN

In order to make the crown larger or smaller follow the same instructions as for making the brim. Slash crown through the middle and insert a piece to make larger or overlap to make smaller. The crown may be lowered or raised in the same manner by adding to or taking from the base.

The styles for crowns change much oftener than they do for brims. For this reason a fashionable hat may become passé simply because the crown is too low or too high for the mode.

RENOVATION AND CARE

To heighten a low crown, remove it from the hat and insert at the base a band of some stiff material, such as buckram or willow, to give the desired height. This, of course, necessitates the use of trimming to cover the band. To lower a high crown, remove several rows of braid from the bottom or cut away the buckram from the top. If the crown is badly worn, it may be removed and a suitable one made from silk or flowers.

RENOVATING MATERIALS

To steam velvet. If hat is soiled, clean it in gasoline or any other solvent such as benzine, chloroform, ether, alcohol, or carbona. Brush velvet thoroughly and remove all threads. Hold it right side up over a kettle of steaming water. Let one person hold it while another brushes against the pile with a firm brush, or place a hot iron upside down with a damp cloth over it. Draw the velvet right side up slowly across the steaming surface, brushing against the pile. Treat velvet ribbon in the same way.

To make panne or mirror velvet. This may be done when an old piece of velvet shows decided creases. After cleaning and steaming velvet place it right side up flat on the board and press it with an iron slowly in the direction of the pile. Continue from one edge of velvet to the other. Do not allow the iron to rest any place or it will leave a mark.

To make brocade or broadtail velvet. If velvet is badly creased, it may be treated to imitate broadtail fur. After cleaning and steaming it, dampen the wrong side with a wet cloth. Fold through the middle lengthwise with pile inside. Two persons then twist and wring it in opposite directions until it is rolled tight. Fasten the two ends to backs of chairs or tack to a board until dry. The surface will have a brocaded effect.

To clean ribbon. It is advisable to use a solvent such as gasoline, provided the work can be done in the open air. There is great danger from fire unless a nonexplosive substance like carbona is used. In case the ribbon will not be injured by water, place it flat on a table and scrub it with mild soapsuds, using a soft scrub brush. Rinse ribbon in several waters, drawing the ribbon through the fingers instead of wringing it. Stretch it on a table or around a smooth bottle or hang it to dry. When it is almost dry press it under a tissue paper or cloth, drawing the ribbon under the iron. Ribbons may be dried without ironing by being wrapped around a smooth bottle or pasted on a mirror or windowpane.

To tint flowers. To rejuvenate slightly faded flowers trim the edges and touch them up with oil, water-color paints, or dye. Use a stiff brush. Velvet flowers may be steamed slightly. The appearance of flowers may be improved in some cases by being veiled with maline.

To improve worn feathers. It is advisable to have feathers renovated by an expert. Ostrich may be improved by steaming if necessary. To recurl, steam the feather, then take three or four flues at one time, beginning at the large end of the feather, and draw them against the back of a knife or any other dull edge with a quick outward-curving stroke.

Glue (preferably milliner's glue or cement) may be used to repair wings, breasts, and other feather trimmings. In some cases it is better to veil them with maline.

To clean lace. Fine and delicate laces which are not too badly soiled may be cleaned with French chalk, corn meal, or magnesia. Cover the lace with French chalk, put it in a fruit jar, shake jar, and allow lace to stand overnight. Shake out all the chalk.

To wash lace, if badly soiled, soak it overnight. Immerse it in mild soapsuds to which may be added ammonia or borax. Squeeze lace to remove dirt. Do not wring it. After rinsing it pin it to an ironing board to dry. Or baste the lace to a piece of cloth face downward before washing, being careful to catch down all the points. After rinsing, partially dry and press it before removing it from the cloth. The lace may be stretched around a bottle to dry. This is a good way to bleach it if it is carefully moistened and put in the sun. With care javelle water may be used to bleach lace. To stiffen lace, rinse it in a mixture of two tablespoons of borax to one cup of water or use one-eighth tablespoon of gum arabic to a cup of water.

To tint lace. If a cream or ecru effect is desired, rinse or soak the lace in tea or carefully strained coffee. Or dissolve oil paint in gasoline and dip the lace. Mix ochre or any color desired with a small quantity of gasoline, strain it, then add it to larger quantity a little at a time until the desired color is obtained.

To clean black lace. Squeeze lace in a mixture of one cup of strong coffee to which has been added one tablespoon of ammonia. Rinse it in a solution of gum arabic and coffee and pin it down or flatten it out on a glass surface.

To clean gold and silver lace. Use alcohol or gasoline. Treat metal ornaments in this way and rub them with chamois.

To freshen veils. Veils should be removed from the hat and rolled when not in use. To cleanse them, wash them in warm soapsuds. Rinse a black veil in tea to which gum arabic has been added (two teaspoons to one pint of water). Stretch it in shape, pin, and dry it over a flat surface.

PART VII. HISTORICAL

CHAPTER XVIII

THE STORY OF THE HAT

Men's Hats
Women's Hats
Significance of Headdress: The Meaning of the Veil—Distinctive Types of Headdress

Any present-day discussion of hats implies that they are to be worn by women. A feminine weakness for headgear is proverbial. The hat stands for all that is frivolous, transitory, and capricious. Cartoonists seldom miss an opportunity to caricature fickle woman and her hat.

Such was not the case in early times, however. For many centuries hats for women were unknown, while men indulged in elaborate styles. They wore hats with long flowing plumes and ornaments richly decorated with gold and silver.

MEN'S HATS

Since men's hats developed long before women's hats, their story must be told here.

The cap was, without doubt, the most ancient form of headdress. Egyptian noblemen wore caps of peculiar shape. Many of them rose high above the head in a helmet effect. They were decorated with symbolic emblems, such as the head of an asp for kingly power, lotus flowers denoting abundance, and sacred feathers which were emblems of sovereignty. In some instances long tabs which indicated authority hung over the chest.

Of all the helmets mentioned in literature, the most memorable is the one worn by Hector. As he parted from Andromache,

THE STORY OF THE HAT

> The babe clung crying to his nurse's breast,
> Scar'd at the dazzling helm and nodding crest.
> . . . .
> And Hector hasted to relieve his child;
> The glittering terror from his brows unbound
> And placed the gleaming helmet on the ground.[1]

The Phrygian bonnet, a cap of classic origin, was worn as late as Anglo-Saxon times. In general outline it resembled a modern stocking cap.

FIG. 113. *Petasus*

So far as is known, the first hat with a brim was the *petasus*, worn by Greek gentlemen when traveling (Fig. 113). This was a small, round hat with a flat crown.

[1] *Iliad*, Book 6, line 9597.

FIG. 114. *Hat with plume — Francis I*

In Chaucer's *Canterbury Tales* mention is made of a merchant wearing "on his head a Flaundrish beaver hat." Before the end of the fourteenth century beaver hats were imported into England.

FIG. 115. *Turban—Charles XIII*

A style of hat fashionable in the fifteenth century was worn by Charles VIII of France (Fig. 115). This was typical of many close-fitting turbans of the time. It is a portrait worth studying for subtle curves of the brim, its excellent proportion, and richly jeweled ornaments. It might be called the forerunner of the modern turban for women. Although its form has changed from time to time, it remains a standard shape.

Francis I of France and Henry VIII of England in the sixteenth century introduced a graceful style with sweeping plume. It has continued one of the most picturesque effects ever used for women's hats (Fig. 114).

During the seventeenth and eighteenth centuries men's hats reached the height of originality. Large hats had a tendency to droop, and accordingly were fastened up to suit the individual, in front, at side

FIG. 116. "*The Slouch Hat*" by Holbein

or back. The three-cornered or "cocked" hat developed from this during the time of William and Mary. Portraits by Holbein, Rembrandt, Hals, and Velaquez show graceful outlines of large hats, many of which were decorated with plumes. This style has become the so-called picture hat for women. (See Fig. 116, page 175, the "Slouch Hat," by Holbein.),

FIG. 117. *Tricorn worn by Napoleon*

Frenchmen of rank both at court and in the army commonly wore plumes on their hats during this period. The famous Gainsborough hat is a direct descendant of this type. The hat gained its name from the English artist, Thomas Gainsborough, who painted beautiful and aristocratic women wearing picture hats.

In the later years of the eighteenth century there appeared a conspicuous style. It was called the stovepipe hat and has come down to us as the conventional dress hat for men. The well-known Puritan hat (Fig. 118) was the prototype of our modern sailor. The cocked hat of George Washington and his generals and the tricorn of Napoleon (Fig. 117) have developed into standard shapes for women's wear.

It was not until the twentieth century that men adopted a few uniform types—the derby, the fedora, the high silk hat, the cap, the regulation straw hat. Even some of these shapes have been appropriated by women for sports wear. For example, the costume of the equestrienne is incomplete without its formal derby or silk hat. The Stetson belongs on the khaki-clad out-of-door girl. Thus, many traditional forms in women's hats are taken from styles that once were worn by men.

FIG. 118. *Puritan hat ("Deacon Chapin" by St. Gaudens)*

WOMEN'S HATS

Egyptian women of high rank wore a close-fitting headdress which rested on an elaborate wig. As shown in Fig. 119, below, sacred symbols, such as the vulture and the asp, formed the decorations.

From the earliest times to the Middle Ages women wore veils or mantles. There are frequent allusions to the veil in all sacred and classical writings. During the eighth, ninth, and tenth centuries it was held in place by a narrow band around the forehead, or by a crown. This crown effect was referred to as a turban.

The forerunner of the turban[1] appeared in the thirteenth century in the form of a close-fitting hat with turned-up brim. It resembled the small white hat worn by American sailors, except that it had a chin strap. The hair was dressed low in a knot at the back of the head and covered with a net caul.

The costume of the fourteenth and fifteenth centuries was characterized by a most eccentric headdress called the hennin.

FIG. 119. *Egyptian*   FIG. 120. *Hennin*

It assumed many forms, the most striking of which was the tall, conical-shaped cap placed far back on the head to which a veil

[1] Two sculptured figures, by Viollet-le-Duc, are shown wearing such turbans on Notre Dame de Chartres.

THE STORY OF THE HAT

was attached (Fig. 120). This distinctive decoration is always associated with fifteenth-century dress and is supposed to reflect the influence of Gothic cathedral spires.

FIG. 121. *Hood—Anne of Brittany*   FIG. 122. *Widow's bonnet—Mary, Queen of Scots*

Anne of Brittany wore a close-fitting bonnet or hood (Fig. 121). It resembled an infant's cap.

Catherine de Medici and Mary, Queen of Scots, each wore widow's mourning bonnets (Fig. 122). They started a custom which still prevails.

During the reign of Louis XIV a peculiar style originated in France. The story goes that the Duchesse de Fontagne while out riding with the king lost her hat. She took her lacy garter and placed it upon her head. This pleased the fancy of the king, and other court ladies adopted the fashion. Hence the name "Fontagne headdress."

Marie Antoinette and her ladies at the court of Louis XVI wore the most fantastic headdress known in history (Fig. 123, page 180). Both in England and in France during this period women's hats were the subject of ridicule. A ship in full sail or a flower garden might rest on a lady's head. It was said that women had to lean their heads out of the cabs because of the extreme height of their headdress.

Immediately following the French Revolution the political and economic reaction was reflected in dress. The simple Empire gown with a poke bonnet gave a new silhouette (Fig. 124, page 181). This modest shape has continued a favorite for children, and is revived from time to time in modified form for women.

FIG. 123. *Eighteenth-century headdress*

A picturesque hat known as the "shepherdess" is used for the frontispiece. This is a portrait of the Empress Eugénie, wife of Napoleon III. As this hat reappears in its various modifications one feature remains constant—a drooping brim in front and back. It is also called a garden hat.

The tam-o'-shanter is a form of cap which owes its name to the hero in one of Burns's poems. It was at first worn by Scottish plowmen and later modified for women and children.

THE STORY OF THE HAT

In the evolution of the hat a few distinct forms appear and all styles are modified from these. The fundamental types are the turban, sailor, picture hat, poke bonnet, tricorn, and mourning

FIG. 124. *Poke bonnet*

or widow's bonnet. The last-named is usually a form of toque. It is similar to a turban except that it has no brim.

There is no hat that cannot be modified from one of these forms.

SIGNIFICANCE OF HEADDRESS

The meaning of the veil. Only veils and mantles are mentioned in the writings of the Hebrews and the Greeks when references are made to women's headdress. The veil throughout history was not primarily for protection but was essentially a symbol. When St. Paul admonished the women to cover their heads in the house of worship, he required this act as a mark of reverence. For the many orders of religious sisterhoods the veil is a badge of humility. It signifies virginity and sacrifice. Modesty and subjection are expressed when the veil is worn by women of India and Persia. The mourning or widow's veil indicates bereavement. Wherever seen, the Red Cross veil is the sign of service. In a similar way the custom of lifting the hat indicates courtesy and service.

The symbolism of the wedding veil is universal in its appeal. While it is a relic of woman's bondage and out of harmony with modern thinking, there is a superstitious reverence for the tradition of purity connected with the wedding veil. This is shown by the custom of throwing it back from the face immediately after the ceremony. It is never to be worn again even though a second marriage occurs. Throughout the centuries it has stood for maidenhood and modesty.

Distinctive types of headdress. There are many kinds of hats which denote rank. Notable examples of these are the king's crown, the cardinal's hat, and the cap or helmet worn by a military officer. The type of headdress serves as a badge for many occupations. Consider the helmet of the fireman, the policeman, the aviator. Again, there is the jockey cap, the cap of the chauffeur, the chef, and the "red cap." Within the house we find the housemaid's cap and the nurse's cap.

The mere mention of dunce's cap or cap and bells calls to mind a wealth of traditions.

Moreover, the type of head covering is often the most distinguishing feature of national costume. No part of it is more

THE STORY OF THE HAT 183

conspicuous than, for example, the Turk's fez, the Highlander's cap, the turban of the Hindu, or the Alpine hat.

Peasant costumes which have remained unchanged for centuries owe much of their picturesqueness to the attractive cap or

FIG. 125. *Dutch cap*

mantle worn. A great variety may be found in different sections of the same country. For example, the stiffly starched Breton cap and the large bow and flowing ends worn by women in Alsace are both entirely unlike the headdress of peasants in Normandy. In the southern countries of Spain, Italy, and

Greece the women favor the mantilla type. This may take the form of a delicately wrought lace scarf or a coarse kerchief. In the Scandinavian and Dutch countries close-fitting caps prevail (Fig. 125, page 183).

The hat or cap of the Quakers and the Shakers is an important part of their costume. It seems to identify these sects and to express their unworldliness. Likewise the conventional poke bonnet on the Salvation Army lassie and the attractive headdress of the Volunteer proclaim religious fervor and service.

One of the strongest traditions related to costume is the academic garb which has survived from medieval times to the present. It is reserved for those of collegiate training. The mortar board has ever stood for educational achievement.

GLOSSARY

Appliqué (pr. á plē kā'). A form of flat trimming made by applying patches of contrasting material with decorative stitches.

Bandeau (pl. bandeaux) (pr. bǎn dō'). Band inserted inside of headsize to make crown fit more closely. Various shapes and materials used both in rigid and in elastic bandeaux.

Base Edge Wire. The wire at the base of crown.

Binding. An edge finish made of bias folds, of strips of braid or ribbon.

Beige (pr. bâzh). Natural tan color, or undyed fabric.

Bow. A knot with a loop or loops.

Brace Wire. Any wire parallel to the edge wire and the headsize.

Cabochon (pr. ká bö shôn'). A convex ornament made of any material used for trimming.

Caul. An ancient form of coarse hair net.

Chapeau (pl. chapeaux) (pr. shȧp pō'). French for hat.

Chenille (pr. shě nēl'). French for caterpillar. Velvety cord used for tassels, braid, and decorative stitches.

Chic (pr. shěk). Denotes originality and taste; cleverness in execution; stylish, or in fashion.

Chiné (pr. shē nā'). Warp-printed. Gives indistinct effect in design. Dresden and Persian designs in ribbon and silk. Often warp-printed.

Chou (pl. choux) (pr. shoō). French for cabbage. Ornament made of ribbon, silk, or velvet.

Ciré (pr. sē rā'). Patent leather effect on ribbon (usually satin), produced by a special process.

Cloche. Bell-shaped hat.

Cockade. A formal rosette made of ribbon.

Commercial. Made in a factory.

Crown Edge Wire. Division wire between tip and side band.

Dresden. Delicate designs usually warp-printed (see chiné) which resemble designs in Dresden china.

Ecru (pr. ā′krōō). Having the color of unbleached linen or of hemp.

Edge Wire. Forms the circumference of the hat.

Facing. A finish for the underside of brim or lining for trimmings. May be made of same or contrasting material. May be bias, straight, or fitted.

Flange. A projecting flat rim or an extension of the brim. The flange may turn back over top of brim or under brim.

Fold. A strip of material, usually bias, applied as a finish and decoration. See Fig. 58, page 97.

Frame. A foundation over which a hat is made. May be of wire, buckram, or other stiff material.

Glacé (pr. glà sā′). Two-toned ribbon or silk. Also applies to a special finish. Glistening or smooth effect.

Gusset. A piece of material inserted to increase flare.

Headsize. The part of the hat which fits next to the hair.

Ligne (pr. lēn′y′). A unit of measurement used to indicate width of ribbon. It is between a sixteenth and an eighth of an inch.

Lingerie (pr. lăn zh′ rē′). Washable. A lace or organdy hat is a lingerie hat. Washable ribbon is lingerie ribbon.

Medallion. A round decorative unit. May or may not be appliquéd.

Moiré (pr. mwä rā′). Watered or clouded effect in ribbon or silk.

Mode. Prevailing style or common fashion.

Mold. A foundation of wood or metal over which a crown may be formed. Molds may also be made of wire for crown or brim, or of stiff paper for brim.

Nouveau (pr. nōō vō′). New. A novelty.

Passé (pr. pä sā′). Past the prime or out of date.

Persian. Reference to designs, printed or woven on silk or ribbon showing Persian influence.

Picot (pr. pē′kō). French for splinter. Small loops on the edge of ribbon.

Plaque (plàk). A flat, round piece of braid or felt used for draping a crown.

Plissé (pr. plē sā′). French for plaited (pleated). Refers to shirred or puckered effect.

GLOSSARY

Plaiting. (a) Interlacing strands of hair, ribbon, straw, etc., to form braid. (b) (pr. plēt ing). A ruffle of material creased in tiny pleats.

Pompadour. Named for Madame Pompadour. Small floral patterns in the French style on ribbon or silk.

Rayon. Manufactured or artificial silk. Also called fiber silk. Made from wood pulp.

Rosette. An ornament usually made of ribbon or lace, gathered or plaited to resemble a rose.

Sash. One or two pieces of ribbon or hemmed silk hanging from the hat.

Side Band. The side of crown or the distance which determines the height of crown.

Shape. An untrimmed hat.

Skeleton Frame. Wire frame with brace wires omitted.

Spoke Wires. The radiating wires which support the edge and brace wires in a brim. Also the perpendicular wires on the side band of crown.

Stitches, Constructive. Chapter x.

Stitches, Decorative. Chapter xiv.

Support Wires. Same as spoke wires.

Tartan. Originally, plaid designs, distinctive of Scottish clans; now, gay plaids in wool or silk cloth or ribbon.

Tête de nêgre (pr. tāt dĕ nĕgr). French for "head of negro." Very dark brown, almost black.

Texture. The surface of a material, as the texture of fur, of taffeta, of net, of leghorn, of felt.

Tip. Top section of crown to which side band is attached.

Tooling. The art of pressing the material with the point of the needle to form a cord around a wire. It is similar to the process of tooling leather.

Vogue. The prevailing fashion.

REFERENCES

TEXTS

AIKEN, CHARLOTTE RANKIN. *The Millinery Department.* 1918.
BEN-YUSUF, MME. ANNA. *The Art of Millinery.* 1909.
LYON, HESTER B. *Modern Millinery.* 1922.
MARTIN, GENE ALLEN. *Make Your Own Hats.* 1921.
REEVE, AMY J. *Practical Home Millinery.* 1912.

JOURNALS

Illustrated Milliner. New York City.
Millinery Trade Review. 1225 Broadway, New York City.

GENERAL

KINNE AND COOLEY. *Shelter and Clothing*, chap. xxiv. 1914.
VAN RENSSALAER, ROSE, AND OTHERS. *Manual of Home Making*, chap. xvi. 1919.

DESIGN

BURBANK, EMILY. *Woman as Decoration.* 1920.
CANFIELD, DOROTHY. *Home Fires in France*, p. 204, "Hats." 1918.
TRAPHAGEN, ETHEL. *Costume Design and Illustration.* 1918.

FABRICS

DENNY, GRACE G. *Fabrics and How to Know Them.* 1922.

THE INDEX

Aigret, 161
Aigrette, 161
Appliqué, 156
Artificial light, effect on color, 8
Artificial silk (rayon), 187
  stitches made with, 159

Baby azure braid, 32
Backstitch, 91
Band trimming of folded points, 132
  See also Stitches, decorative; Trimmings
Bandeau, 26
Bands:
  bias band for side band, 79, 80
  cutting curved side band, 22
  cutting straight side band, 21
  for soft crowns, 51, 79, 80
  joining plain band and gathered tip, 23
  joining tip and side band, 22, 80
  sewing to headsize, 19
Beaver, 40
Beaver cloth, 37
Belgian split braid, 32
Bias:
  cutting, 46, 95, 96
  joining, 97
Bias folds. *See* Folds, bias
Binding, 95, 185
  brim covering and, 101
  ribbon or braid, 100
  silk or organdy, 100
  velvet or silk, 86
Bird's nest braid, 32
Blanket stitch, 156
Bows, 123–129, 185
  aigrette, 127
  Alsatian, 126
  art in making, 123
  butterfly, 128
  tailored, 124
  tied or cravat, 125
  wiring, 124
Brace wire, 59, 62, 185
Braids:
  combining silk and, 86
  covering brims with, 85
  extending from edge, 86
  frames for, 84
  hats covered with, 83–90
  kinds, 32–37
  preparation of, 84
  sewing, 83
  underfacing with, 86
Brim coverings:
  estimating materials, 70, 71
  materials for. *See* Fabrics; Frames
  measurements for, 70
  sewing braid over wire mold, 89
  removal of braid, 90
  See also Fabrics· Folds; Materials, estimation of
Brims:
  attaching to crown, 82
  finishing edges. *See* Edge finishes
  halo, 117, 118
  measurements, 10, 11, 15, 70
  molded:
    crinoline, 48
    edge binding and finishing, 45, 47
    placing pattern on willow, 43
    preparation of materials, 43
    shaping, 45
    upturning, 46
    without patterns, 46
  mushroom, 59
  paper patterns:
    construction, 18, 19
    copying, 10, 15
    cutting, 13, 18
      headsize of, 13, 14
    designing, 16
    drooping slightly, 17
    even, 16
    headsize, sewing to band, 19
    irregular-shaped, 18
    joining to crown, 24
    measuring, 10, 11, 15, 70
    uneven, 16
    upturning, 17
  tucked, 116
  underfacings for. *See* Underfacings
  wire:
    brace wire of, 59, 62, 185
    drooping, 59
    headsize for, 55, 56
    irregular-shaped, 62
    measurements for, 54, 61, 62, 63

Brims, wire (*continued*):
   sailor, 58
   support or spoke wires for, 56
   upturning, 60, 61
Broadcloth, 37
Buckram, 26

Cable cord, 26
Candle wicking, 26
Cape net, 26
Care of hats, 166 ff.
Catch stitch, 91, 157
Catstitch, 91, 157
Cellophane braid, 34
Cement, 28
Chain stitch, 157
Character in a hat, 1 ff.
Chenille trimmings, 34, 137
Chiffon, 37
Child's hats, 118
   poke bonnet, 180
   tam-o'-shanter, 120 ff., 180
China Milan braid, 32
Chip braid, 34
Choice of a hat, 1 ff.
   contour and coloring considered, 3
   cost limits, 3
   difficulty in, 2
Chroma, 6
Clamps, 26
Cockades, 130–134, 185
Color, 5 ff.
   artificial light's effect on, 8
   chroma, 6
   complement, 7, 8
   constants, 7
   cool, 6
   harmony of, 7, 8
   hue, 7, 8
   tint, 7
   use of chart for, 7
   value, 6
   warm, 6
Coney, 40
Copying brims, 10, 15
Cord trimmings, 134. *See also* Cords
Cords:
   brims:
      edged with, 110, 111
      finished with, 104
      made of, 112
      underfacing of, 111
   crowns finished with, 82, 110
   trimming with, 104
Couching stitch, 157

Covering frames, 64, 69, 72, 73. *See also* Brim coverings; Coverings, hat; Crown coverings; Crowns, covering
Covering irregular shapes, 76, 77
Coverings, hat:
   braids, 32–37, 83–90
   estimating materials for, 70 ff.
   fabrics, 37–40
   for brim, 64, 70–77. *See also* Brim coverings
   for crown, 72. *See also* Crown coverings
   furs, 40–41
   of one material, 77
   See also Fabrics; Materials, estimation of; Velvet
Crêpe, 37
Crêpe de Chine, 37
Crewel stitch, 158
Crinoline, 26
Crocheting, 157
Cross-stitch, 157
Crown coverings:
   bias folds, 109
   braids. *See* Braids
   draped, 88
   estimating materials for, 70, 71, 72
   folds with wired cord, 110
   for child's stitched hat, 120
   of one material, 77
   ribbon, 111, 112
   sectional, 82, 88
   silk, 115
   See also Fabrics; Materials, estimation of
Crowns, 48
   band for soft crown, 51
   band with soft tip, 52
   band with stiff tip, 51
   changing style of, 168
   covering, 78 ff., 110
      attaching to brim, 82
      crown in two pieces, 79
      finishing at base, 82
      sectional, 82
      smooth-covered, 78
      soft, 80, 81
   draped, 88
   molded:
      materials, 48
      mold for, 49
         stretching material on, 50
      wire, 66
   soft, of crinoline, 51
   wiring base edge of, 51

THE INDEX

paper patterns for:
  construction of, 22 ff.
  cutting, 21, 22
  designing, 21
  in one piece, 24
  joining brim and crown, 24
  joining plain band and gathered tip, 23
  joining tip and side band, 22
  measuring, 21
  sectional, making, 23
sectional, 82, 88
tam-o'-shanter, 88, 120 ff.
tips. *See* Tips
wire:
  construction of, 67, 68, 69
  covering mold for, 64, 69, 72
  measurements for, 66
  molds for, 66
  See also Frames

Darning stitch, 157
Dominant harmony, 7
Duck cloth, 28
Duck feathers, 161
Duvetyn, 37
Dye, 28

Edge finishes, 47, 95 ff., 110, 111, 116
  bias fold, 98, 99, 101
  bindings, 45, 100, 101
  cord, 104, 110
  folds:
    stretching, 98
    without wire, 99
    See also Folds
  plain:
    drooping, 102
    maline, 102
    upturning, 102
  sectional facings, 103
  shirred edge, 102
  wiring, 45, 47, 74
Edge wire, 45, 47, 58, 74, 186
Egret, 161
Equipment, materials for, 26–31
Ermine, 40
Estimation of materials. *See* Materials, estimation of

Fabrics, kinds of, 37–40
Facing, 186
  sectional, 103
  with velvet, 74
  See also Underfacing

Facing line, 62
Faille, 37
Feathers:
  kinds of, 161–163
  laws governing use of, in the United States, 160
  renovating, 170
Felt, 37
Flange, 95, 186
Flower and fruit trimmings, 138 ff.
  parts of, making, 134, 135
  to tint, 170
Folds, 186
  bias, 95
    crown of, 109
    decorated, 108, 109
    extending from edge, 101
    on edge of brim, 98, 99
    soft hats of, 107
  drooping, 102
  estimating width, 98
  finishing, 99
  flat, 97
  French, 97
  made before attaching, 99
  maline, 102
  on edge of brim, 98
  on edge, without wire, 99
  simulated, 92
  upturned, 102
Fowls, feathers of, 161
Frames:
  molded, 42 ff.
    free-hand, 46
    headsize band, 44
    headsize wiring, 44
    materials for, 43
    molding willow over paper, 66
    reshaping, 168
    See also Brims, molded; Crowns, molded
  wire, 53 ff.
    construction, 55
    covering, 64, 69, 72, 73
    for shirred hat, 114
    materials for, 54
    measurements for making, 54, 61, 62, 63, 66
    molding willow over wire, 64
    molds:
      preparing, 64
      wire crown, 66
    reshaping, 168
    See also Brims, wire; Crowns, wire
French knots, 157

Fruit and flower trimmings, 138 ff.
Furs, kinds of, 40

Gathering stitch, 92
Georgette, 38
Gingham, 38
Glue, 28
Goose feathers, 161
Gourah feathers, 161
Grebe feathers, 162
Grosgrain, 38
Guinea feathers, 162

Hair braid, 34
Hair line, 62
Halo brims, 117, 118
Handling the hat, 166
Harmony, dominant, 7
Hatter's plush, 38
Headdress:
  denoting rank or occupation, 182
  men's, historical, 172–177
  significance of, 182–184
  women's, historical, 178–181
Headsize, 11, 186
  cutting, 13–15
  for molded frames, 43 f.
  for wire frames, 55 f.
  measuring, 11
  wiring, 44, 55
Hemming stitch, 92
Hemp braid, 34
Hemstitching on silk hat, 115
Heron feathers, 162
Herringbone stitch, 158
Hue, 7, 8

Intensity of color, 6

Knot or snail or running chain stitch, 158

Lace:
  to clean, 170, 171
  to tint, 171
Lacing stitch, 92
Lacquer, 28
Lazy-daisy stitch, 158
Leaf stitch, 158
Leather, 38
Leghorn, 35
  to alter brim, 167
  to clean, 167
Ligne, 39, 186

Linings, directions for making, 164
  French, 165
  plain, 164
  tailored, 165
Liséré braid, 34

Maline, 38
  folds of, 102
Marabou, 162
Materials:
  estimation of:
    for brims, 70, 71
    for crowns, 71, 72
  for construction, 26–31
  for decoration. *See* Coverings, hat; Fabrics; Trimmings
  for hat coverings, 70–77
Measurements:
  for brims, 10, 11, 15, 70
  for crowns, 21, 60
  for wire frames, 54, 61, 62, 63, 66
Messaline, 38
Metal cloth, 38
Milan braid, 35
  to freshen, 167
Milan hemp, 35
Milliner's fold, 97
Mink, 40
Mold, 186
  buckram wired, 49
  crown, stretching material on, 50
  for irregular shape, 62
  paper, 19, 20
  removing brim from, 90
  wire, sewing braid over, 89
  wooden, 31, 49
  See also Frames, molded
Molds, wire crown, 66
Mole, 40
Monkey fur, 41
Mushroom brim, 59

Net, 38
  cape, 36
  flexible or elastic, 28
  rice, 29
Novelty trimmings, 35, 134
Numidi, 162

Oilcloth, 38
Organdy, 38
Ostrich:
  feathers, 162
  tip, 163
  to curl and freshen, 170

Ottoman, 38
Outline stitch, 158

Panama braid, 35
  to clean, 167
Panama cloth, 28
Paper brim construction, 18 ff.
Paper crown construction, 22 ff.
Paper for patterns, 29
Paper patterns, how to make, 10–25.
  See also Brims; Crowns
Paradise feathers, 162
Parrakeet feathers, 162
Parrot feathers, 162
Peacock feathers, 162
Peau de soie, 38
Pheasant feathers, 162
Plaque, 186
  covering brim with, 86
  for tam-o'-shanter, 88
  tagal, 36
Pliers, 29
Plush, hatter's, 38
Primary hues, 7
Pyroxlin, 35

Quills, 154, 163

Rayon, 159, 187
Renovation and care, 166 ff.
  freshening straw hats, 167
  renovating materials, 169–171
  reshaping frames, 168
  varying style of crown, 168
Ribbon:
  kinds, 38
  to clean, 169
Ribbon bows, 123 ff.
Ribbon cockade, 130
Ribbon hats, 110 ff.
Rosette, 128, 134, 187
Running chain stitch, 158
Running stitch, 92

Sailor hat, 58, 181
Satin, 39
Satin stitch, 159
Seal, 41
Sealing-wax trimmings, 137
Secondary hues, 7
Sectional crowns, 23, 24, 82, 88
Sectional facings, 103
Seed stitch, 159
Shirred hat, 113

Side band, 187. *See also* Bands
Silk hats:
  of strips of silk or ribbon, 110
  shirred, 113
  stitched or hemstitched, 115
  with tucked brim, 116
Simulated fold, 92
Slip hemming, 92
Slip stitch, 93
Snail stitch, 158
Sports hat, 106 ff.
Squirrel, 41
Stab stitch, 93
Steaming, device for, 28
Stem stitch, 158
Stitched hat, 115, 118
Stitches:
  construction, 91
    kinds of, 91–94
  decorative, 156
    kinds of, 156–159
    use of, 156
Straw hats, renovating, 167
Support or spoke wires, 56, 187
Swinging tack, 93

Taffeta, 39
Tagal braid, 36
Tam-o'-shanter, 180
  making, 120, 121
  plaque for making, 88
Tarlatan, 29
Test of a becoming hat, 4
  color harmony, 5
  outline, importance of, 5
Texture, 5, 9, 187
Tie tack, 93
Timbo braid, 36
Tinting:
  flowers, 171
  lace, 172
Tints, 7
Tip, ostrich, 163
Tips, 187
  covering, 79
  cutting, 79
  for soft crowns, 80, 81
  gathered, joining to band, 23
  joining to side band, 22, 80
  of shirred hats, 114
  soft band with, 52
  stiff band with, 51
Tommy iron, 29
Tooling, 75, 187

Tools, 29
Trimmings, 123–155
  cord, 104
  for child's stitched hat, 120
Tulle, 40
Turkey feathers, 163
Tuscan braid, 36

Underfacing:
  for irregular shapes, 77
  for stitched hat, 115
  of radiating strips, 111
  of yarn surface, 110
  sectional, 103
  with braid, 86
  with velvet, 74

Van Dyck collars, influence on shape of hat, 2
Veil, 8
  origin of, 178
  significance of, 182
  to freshen, 171
Veiling, 40

Velours, 40
Velvet:
  covering frame with, 72 ff., 76 f.
  kinds of, 40
  to make brocade or broadtail, 169
  to make panne or mirror, 169
  to steam, 169
  underfacing with, 74
Visca braid, 36
Vulture feathers, 163

Willow, 30
  cutting, 43
  molding over paper, 66
  molding over wire, 64
Willow plumes, 163
Wire, kinds of, 30

Yarn:
  trimmings, 136 ff.
  underfacing of, 110
Yedda braid, 37

Zipper braid, 37

CPSIA information can be obtained at www.ICGtesting.com
Printed in the USA
LVOW071358261012